Ephesians, Philippians, Colossians

LIVING WITH FAITHFULNESS AND JOY

BRIAN HARBOUR
RAY POLLARD
RONNIE & RENATE HOOD
JOE CALDWELL

BAPTISTWAYPRESS®

Dallas, Texas

Ephesians, Philippians, Colossians—Adult Bible Study Guide—Large Print Edition

Copyright © 2008 by BAPTISTWAY PRESS®.

All rights reserved.
Printed in the United States of America.

BAPTISTWAY PRESS® Management Team
Executive Director, Baptist General Convention of Texas: Randel Everett
Director, Missions, Evangelism, and Ministry Team: Wayne Shuffield
Ministry Team Leader: Phil Miller
Publisher, BAPTISTWAY PRESS®: Ross West

Cover and Interior Design and Production: Desktop Miracles, Inc.
Printing: Data Reproductions Corporation

First edition: September 2008

ISBN–13: 978–1–934731–15–4

How to Make the Best Use of This Issue

Whether you're the teacher or a student—

1. Start early in the week before your class meets.

2. Overview the study. Review the table of contents and read the study introduction. Try to see how each lesson relates to the overall study.

3. Use your Bible to read and consider prayerfully the Scripture passages for the lesson. (You'll see that each writer has chosen a favorite translation for the lessons in this issue. You're free to use the Bible translation you prefer and compare it with the translation chosen for that unit, of course.)

4. After reading all the Scripture passages in your Bible, then read the writer's comments. The comments are intended to be an aid to your study of the Bible.

5. Read the small articles—"sidebars"—in each lesson. They are intended to provide additional, enrichment information and inspiration and to encourage thought and application.

6. Try to answer for yourself the questions included in each lesson. They're intended to encourage further thought and application, and they can also be used in the class session itself.

If you're the teacher—

A. Do all of the things just mentioned, of course. As you begin the study with your class, be sure to find a way to help your class know the date on which each lesson will be studied. You might do this in one or more of the following ways:

- In the first session of the study, briefly overview the study by identifying with your class the date on which each lesson will be studied. Lead your class to write the date in the table of contents on page 9 and on the first page of each lesson.

- Make and post a chart that indicates the date on which each lesson will be studied.

- If all of your class has e-mail, send them an e-mail with the dates the lessons will be studied.

- Provide a bookmark with the lesson dates. You may want to include information about your church and then use the bookmark as a visitation tool, too.

- Develop a sticker with the lesson dates, and place it on the table of contents or on the back cover.

B. Get a copy of the *Teaching Guide*, a companion piece to this *Study Guide*. The *Teaching Guide* contains additional Bible comments plus two teaching plans. The teaching plans in the *Teaching Guide* are intended to provide practical, easy-to-use teaching suggestions that will work in your class.

C. After you've studied the Bible passage, the lesson comments, and other material, use the teaching suggestions in the *Teaching Guide* to help you develop your plan for leading your class in studying each lesson.

D. You may want to get the additional adult Bible study comments—*Adult Online Bible Commentary*—by Dr. Jim Denison, pastor of Park Cities Baptist Church, Dallas, Texas, that are available at www.baptistwaypress.org and can be downloaded free. An additional teaching plan plus teaching resource items are also available at www.baptistwaypress.org.

E. You also may want to get the enrichment teaching help that is provided on the internet by the *Baptist Standard* at www.baptiststandard.com. (Other class participants may find this information helpful, too.) Call 214–630–4571 to begin your subscription to the printed edition of the *Baptist Standard*.

F. Enjoy leading your class in discovering the meaning of the Scripture passages and in applying these passages to their lives.

Writers of This Study Guide

Brian Harbour wrote lessons 1–4 on Ephesians. After serving as a pastor for forty-one years, Dr. Harbour retired from First Baptist Church, Richardson, Texas, to develop the Harbour Leadership Center and to establish a non-profit organization called SeminaryPLUS, which is devoted to coaching and encouraging pastors (see www.seminaryplus.org). He continues to serve as a board member of the Baylor Health Care System Board and is an adjunct professor at Dallas Baptist University. He has also served as the Winfred Moore Visiting Professor in the Department of Religion at Baylor University.

Ray Pollard of Burlington, North Carolina, formerly of Midlothian, Virginia, wrote lessons 5–7 on Ephesians. Now retired, Dr. Pollard has served as pastor of churches in Tennessee, North Carolina, and Virginia, and on the staff of the Virginia Baptist General Board. He has written three previous series of lessons for *Adult Bible Study Guide*.

Ronnie and Renate Hood wrote lessons 8–11 on Philippians. Dr. Ronnie W. Hood II is senior pastor of Fellowship Baptist Church, Longview, Texas, and serves on the Executive Board of the Baptist General

Convention of Texas. He is a graduate of Samford University, Birmingham, Alabama. Dr. Renate Viveen Hood is associate professor of Biblical Studies and Greek at LeTourneau University, Longview, Texas. She earned medical science degrees in the Netherlands. The Hoods studied at New Orleans Baptist Theological Seminary, where Ronnie earned M.Div., Th.M., and Ph.D. (Church History) degrees, and Renate earned M.Div. and Ph.D. (Biblical Studies and Greek) degrees.

Joe Caldwell, writer of the *Study Guide* materials on Colossians, has served as pastor of churches in Texas and California and for six years as an active duty United States Army Chaplain. He currently serves on the staff of Golden Gate Baptist Theological Seminary in California and is a Ph.D. student in New Testament Studies there. He also teaches Spiritual Formation as an adjunct professor at Golden Gate.

EPHESIANS, PHILIPPIANS, COLOSSIANS: Living with Faithfulness and Joy

DATE OF STUDY

UNIT ONE
Ephesians

Introducing

EPHESIANS, PHILIPPIANS, COLOSSIANS: *Living with Faithfulness and Joy*

But How?

To live with faithfulness and joy—isn't that what at our best we want to do? But how? These lessons from the Letters to the Ephesians, the Philippians, and the Colossians are designed to help us do that. In fact, the lessons flow naturally out of these letters, for that theme is a major emphasis of these letters looked at together.

The Prison Epistles

These letters, along with the small Letter to Philemon, are sometimes called the "prison epistles." They are called the "prison epistles" because references to Paul as a prisoner appear in each of them (see Ephesians 3:1; 4:1; Philippians 1; Colossians 4:10; Philemon 1, 9, 13, 23).

The Book of Acts indicates that Paul was in prison for an extended period of time in Caesarea (Acts 24) and in Rome (Acts 28). The traditional view is that the prison of the "prison epistles" was in Rome. Knowing the situation in Paul's life when he wrote these letters provides help in interpreting and understanding them.

This Series of Lessons

Even though the "prison epistles" include Philemon, we will focus only on Ephesians, Philippians, and Colossians during this study. One major reason is that an abundance of useful insights can be found in Ephesians, Philippians, and Colossians. Another is that we had an opportunity to study Philemon recently in our BaptistWay Press curriculum plan.[1] Therefore, we will focus only on Ephesians, Philippians, and Colossians during this study.

An additional factor in the development of these lessons is the desire to avoid repeating passages of Scripture that are too similar. Colossians and Ephesians, for example, share some similar content. This fact can be seen readily by comparing Colossians 3 with Ephesians 4:17—6:9. Therefore, the common content is studied only once, in the Ephesians study.

The lessons in the three units thus serve at least two purposes. They provide a guide to study of the books themselves, beginning with the context of each book and moving sequentially through each of them. They also provide guidance for truly "living with faithfulness and joy." May we learn to do both as we study the passages of Scripture in these lessons.

UNIT ONE. EPHESIANS

UNIT TWO. PHILIPPIANS

UNIT THREE. COLOSSIANS

Additional Resources for Studying Ephesians, Philippians, Colossians: Living with Faithfulness and Joy [2]

EPHESIANS

F.F. Bruce. *Colossians, Philemon, and Ephesians.* New International Commentary on the New Testament. Grand Rapids, Michigan: Eerdmans Publishing Company, 1984.

Craig S. Keener. *IVP Bible Background Commentary: New Testament.* Downers Grove, Illinois: InterVarsity Press, 1993.

Andrew T. Lincoln. *Ephesians.* Word Biblical Commentary. Volume 42. Dallas, Texas: Word Books, Publisher, 1990.

Ralph P. Martin. "Ephesians." *The Broadman Bible Commentary.* Volume 11. Nashville, Tennessee: Broadman Press, 1971.

Pheme Perkins. "The Letter to the Ephesians." *The New Interpreter's Bible.* Volume XI. Nashville, Tennessee: Abingdon Press, 2000.

A. T. Robertson. *Word Pictures in the New Testament.* Volume IV. Nashville, Tennessee: Broadman Press, 1931.

PHILIPPIANS

Fred B. Craddock. *Philippians.* Interpretation: A Bible Commentary for Teaching and Preaching. Atlanta: John Knox Press, 1985.

Gerald F. Hawthorne. *Philippians.* Word Biblical Commentary. Volume 43. Waco, Texas: Word Books Publisher, 1983.

Morna D. Hooker. "The Letter to the Philippians." *The New Interpreter's Bible.* Volume XI. Nashville, Tennessee: Abingdon Press, 2000.

Craig S. Keener. *IVP Bible Background Commentary: New Testament.* Downers Grove, Illinois: InterVarsity Press, 1993.

Ralph P. Martin. *Philippians.* Revised edition. The Tyndale New Testament Commentaries. Grand Rapids, Michigan: William B. Eerdmans Publishing Company, 1987.

A. T. Robertson. *Word Pictures in the New Testament.* Volume IV. Nashville, Tennessee: Broadman Press, 1931.

Frank Stagg. "Philippians." *The Broadman Bible Commentary.* Volume 11. Nashville, Tennessee: Broadman Press, 1971.

COLOSSIANS

F.F. Bruce. *Colossians, Philemon, and Ephesians.* New International Commentary on the New Testament. Grand Rapids, Michigan: Eerdmans, 1984.

James D.G. Dunn. *The Epistles to the Colossians and to Philemon.* The New International Greek Testament Commentary. Grand Rapids, Michigan: William B. Eerdmans Publishing Co., 1996.

David E. Garland. *Colossians, Philemon*. The NIV Application Commentary. Grand Rapids, Michigan: Zondervan Publishing House, 1998.

Craig S. Keener. *IVP Bible Background Commentary: New Testament*. Downers Grove, Illinois: InterVarsity Press, 1993.

Andrew T. Lincoln. "The Letter to the Colossians." *The New Interpreter's Bible*. Volume XI. Nashville, Tennessee: Abingdon Press, 2000.

Ralph P. Martin. *Ephesians, Colossians, Philemon*. Interpretation: A Bible Commentary for Teaching and Preaching. Atlanta: John Knox Press, 1991.

Richard R. Melick, Jr. *Philippians, Colossians, Philemon*. The New American Commentary, Volume 32. Nashville, Tennessee: Broadman Press, 1991.

A. T. Robertson. *Word Pictures in the New Testament*. Volume IV. Nashville, Tennessee: Broadman Press, 1931.

R.E.O. White. "Colossians." *The Broadman Bible Commentary*. Volume 11. Nashville, Tennessee: Broadman Press, 1971.

NOTES

1. See the study on *1 and 2 Timothy, Titus, and Philemon*.

2. Listing a book does not imply full agreement by the writers or BAPTISTWAY PRESS® with all of its comments.

The Letter to the Ephesians

Ephesus, the original destination for the Letter to the Ephesians, was a leading city in the Roman province of Asia Minor, which geographically is part of modern Turkey. Many Bible students, however, consider Ephesians to have been intended for the church as a whole, not just the church at Ephesus specifically.

The letter is rich in content about how to live in faithfulness to Christ. It begins with a broad, majestic view of what God has done in Christ (Ephesians 1—3) and continues with directions for living in the real world in response to what God has done (Eph. 4—6).

In the letter's first-century context, one of its great concerns was helping Gentile and Jewish Christians realize that through God's grace "the dividing wall, that is, the hostility between us" had been "broken down" (Ephesians 2:14).[1] That's still good news in our broken world, to know that God in Christ can bring reconciliation between people.

Too, today even those who like the Gentiles once were "aliens" and "strangers" (2:11) can now be "citizens with the saints and also members of the household of God" (2:19). That means you, too.

UNIT ONE. EPHESIANS

Lesson 1	Get in Line with God's Plan	Ephesians 1:1–14
Lesson 2	Celebrate the Difference God Makes	Ephesians 2:1–10
Lesson 3	Cherish All in the Family	Ephesians 2:11–21
Lesson 4	Open Yourself to All God Has for You	Ephesians 3:14–21
Lesson 5	Grow Up into Christ—Together	Ephesians 4:1–16
Lesson 6	Follow the Directions	Ephesians 4:17—5:2, 11–16
Lesson 7	Be Christian in Family Relationships	Ephesians 5:21—6:4

NOTES

1. Unless otherwise indicated, all Scripture quotations in lessons 1–4 are from the New International Version. In lessons 5–7 and this unit introduction, all Scripture quotations unless otherwise indicated are from the New Revised Standard Version.

FOCAL TEXT
Ephesians 1:1–14

BACKGROUND
Ephesians 1

LESSON ONE

Get in Line with God's Plan

MAIN IDEA

God calls us to participate in the lavish plan he has set forth in Christ for enjoying all the blessings of being in good standing in God's family.

QUESTION TO EXPLORE

What has God done for us in Christ, and why does it matter?

STUDY AIM

To describe God's plan for human life and respond to God's offer

QUICK READ

The Holy Spirit will enable we who are in Christ to claim the generous provisions God makes available to us.

chap. 3
v. 1

I remember hearing a few years back about a famous golfer who flew to a Middle Eastern country to play golf with the king of that particular country and some of his special friends. The king sent his private jet to bring the famous golfer to his palace, and he entertained his guest royally while he was there.

As the golfer boarded the plane to come home, the king told him he wanted to give him a gift for his kindness in coming to play with him and his friends. The golfer protested, but the king insisted. "What would you like as a gift?" the king persistently asked. Finally the golfer relented and told the king that he could always use another golf club. With that he boarded the plane and headed home.

Weeks passed, and no gift came from the king. All the while the golfer fantasized about what kind of club the king would send. Perhaps he would send a jewel-studded putter or a driver crafted just for him. Finally, the golfer received in the mail an envelope from the king. Confused about how that envelope could hold his long-awaited golf club, the golfer ripped open the envelope and discovered a deed to a beautiful country club nearby that sported the most spectacular golf course of the region. The golfer expected a golf *club* but the king gave him a *Golf Club*.

I don't know whether the story is true, but it nevertheless serves as a parable of our lives. Most of us live beneath our privileges as Christians. To use the language of the story, we settle for an individual golf *club* when

God really wants us to have a *Golf Club*. No passage in the New Testament so clearly identifies what God wants to give each of us as Christians as the opening verses of Paul's Letter to the Ephesians.

EPHESIANS 1:1–14

1Paul, an apostle of Christ Jesus by the will of God,

To the saints in Ephesus, the faithful in Christ Jesus:

2Grace and peace to you from God our Father and the Lord Jesus Christ.

3Praise be to the God and Father of our Lord Jesus Christ, who has blessed us in the heavenly realms with every spiritual blessing in Christ. **4**For he chose us in him before the creation of the world to be holy and blameless in his sight. In love **5**he predestined us to be adopted as his sons through Jesus Christ, in accordance with his pleasure and will— **6**to the praise of his glorious grace, which he has freely given us in the One he loves. **7**In him we have redemption through his blood, the forgiveness of sins, in accordance with the riches of God's grace **8**that he lavished on us with all wisdom and understanding. **9**And he made known to us the mystery of his will according to his good pleasure, which he purposed in Christ, **10**to be put into effect when the times will have reached their fulfillment—to bring all things in heaven and on earth together under one head, even Christ.

11 In him we were also chosen, having been predestined according to the plan of him who works out everything in conformity with the purpose of his will, **12** in order that we, who were the first to hope in Christ, might be for the praise of his glory. **13** And you also were included in Christ when you heard the word of truth, the gospel of your salvation. Having believed, you were marked in him with a seal, the promised Holy Spirit, **14** who is a deposit guaranteeing our inheritance until the redemption of those who are God's possession—to the praise of his glory.

The Promise (1:1–3)

After the introduction of his Letter to the Ephesians, Paul presented a remarkable picture of God as a father "who has blessed us in the heavenly realms with every spiritual blessing in Christ" (Ephesians 1:3). How distorted at times is our picture of God. We often think of God as a tyrant who capriciously moves us around like checkers on a board. Or we picture God as a judge with a long stick ready to rap us on the shoulder any time we get out of line. Or we understand God to be an impersonal force to whom we cannot relate in a personal way. Or we consider God a distant proprietor who is not really concerned.

These commonly held concepts of God are not the biblical picture of God. Paul picked up on the picture of God given by Jesus himself, who called God our Father. God is not a tyrant, a judge, an impersonal force, or a distant supervisor. He is our Father who wants to bless us.

How can we experience God's blessing? The blessing God provides can be ours "in Christ" (Eph. 1:3). To experience the blessing of God in our lives, we must be in a relationship with Christ, and we must also be in fellowship with Christ. God wants to enrich our lives with his blessings. That's the kind of God he is. But God cannot do this when we are apart from Christ or out of fellowship with Christ, for Christ is the one through whom God's blessings are supplied. How do we know that God is this kind of God? We know because of what God has provided for us through Jesus Christ in the process of salvation.

The Provision (1:4–12)

Paul did not leave us to guess about what God wants to provide us. Instead, Paul described God's provision in elaborate detail.

The Apostle announced that God "chose us in him before the creation of the world" (1:4). Salvation is not something we do for God. Salvation is a gift from God. God takes the initiative in the process of salvation. He "chose us." Jesus presented a similar idea in John 6:44: "No one can come to me unless the Father who sent me draws him." We do not provide our own salvation; God does.

In addition, God "predestined us to be adopted as his sons" (Eph. 1:5). The idea of adoption is one of the most beautiful New Testament pictures of what God has done for us. When a person was adopted in the ancient world, he had all the rights of a legitimate son in his own family, and he completely lost all rights in his old family. In the eyes of the law, an adopted son was a new person. In fact, so new was he that even all debts and obligations connected with his previous family were canceled out as if they had never existed. That pictures what God has done for us. He adopted us into his forever family, giving us all the rights in his family. He then canceled out all our past and made us new persons.

Paul added that God also redeemed us. He wrote: "In him we have redemption through his blood" (1:7). "Redemption" comes from a word that means *to ransom*, a word from the slave market. A slave on sale was powerless to liberate himself, because he was under an obligation he himself could never pay. However, when someone paid a ransom for him, the slave was released to go with his new owner. That is what God did for us. He bought us on the slave market of sin, and he set us free.

Further, in Christ, God also forgave us: "In him we have . . . the forgiveness of sins" (1:7). "Forgiveness" can be translated *dismissed*. That is, God has dismissed our sins. They have been set aside and are no longer taken into account. The word translated "forgiveness" can also be translated *to carry away*. This is a reference to the scapegoat used on the Day of Atonement (Leviticus 16). Every year, the high priest would take a goat, transfer to that goat all the sins of the people, and send the goat out into the wilderness, symbolizing the carrying away of their sins. God forgave us and redeemed us.

Finally, Paul declared that God "made known to us the mystery of his will" (Eph.1:9). "Mystery" does not mean something mysterious or weird. It means a *sacred secret*, once hidden but now revealed to God's people. The mystery about which Paul spoke was the mystery of God's plan for humankind. God has a plan for our world. This plan is something no course of instruction, no university curriculum, and no scientific investigation will ever discover. God had to reveal this plan to us.

Here is God's plan: Jesus came into the world to wipe out the divisions, to remove the tensions, and to close the gaps that separate us from God and from others. God wants to bring all people and all things together as one. Through salvation we not only learn about this plan, but we also have a part in the implementation of the plan.

Through the process of salvation, God has chosen us, adopted us, redeemed us, forgiven us, and then revealed to us his will. We know that God is a God who wants to bless us because of what God has done for us in Christ through the process of salvation.

But how do we know all these things have occurred? How do we know that we have been chosen, adopted, redeemed, and forgiven? How do we know that God has revealed his will to us? How do we know that salvation is for real? We know these things because they have been confirmed by the Holy Spirit in our lives.

The Prompter (1:13–14)

What does the Holy Spirit do in our lives? Paul referred to the two-fold work of the Holy Spirit in our hearts.

In the *present,* the Holy Spirit seals us. A "seal" served four purposes in the ancient world. First, a seal was used to guarantee the genuine character of a document, as a notary public today uses his or her seal to guarantee the genuineness of a signature. That is what the Holy Spirit does. As the Holy Spirit comes into our lives and lives in us, he gives evidence we are genuine Christians.

Second, a seal was used to mark ownership as we do when we put the names on our children's clothes as they go off to camp. That is what the Holy Spirit does. As the Holy Spirit comes into our lives and lives in us, he marks us as belonging to Christ.

Third, a seal was used to protect against tampering or harm as we do today by putting locks on boxes. That is what the Holy Spirit does. As the Holy Spirit comes into our lives and lives in us, he keeps us from being tampered with by Satan. He protects us.

Fourth, a seal was used to indicate the transaction was completed as we do today when we put our signature on a document. That is what the Holy Spirit does. As the Holy Spirit comes into our lives and lives in us, he reminds us that our redemption is complete. The deal has been cut. We now belong to God.

Right now, in the life of every believer, the Holy Spirit is giving assurance that all these things are true. As Paul put it in his Roman epistle, "The Spirit himself testifies with our spirit that we are God's children" (Romans 8:16). ✗

In the *future*, the Holy Spirit will complete the work of God in our lives. The presence of the Holy Spirit in our lives points to the future God has for us, for the Holy Spirit is "a deposit guaranteeing our inheritance" (1:14). The Greek word for "deposit" means the *earnest money* on the purchase of something. It means the *down payment* or *first installment*. The Holy Spirit is the earnest money or down payment that guarantees the full payment of our inheritance in the future.

This inheritance may be a reference to our resurrection body that will be provided for us at death, a resurrection body that is adequate for our new existence in the life to come. Or this inheritance may be a reference to the place ✗ prepared for us in heaven, a place Jesus said he would prepare specifically for us (John 14:1–3). Or this inheritance may be a symbol of the eternal fellowship we will have with God and with the children of God through all eternity.

The Holy Spirit provides the assurance *now* that we will eventually receive our inheritance *in the future*. Because of what the Holy Spirit does for us now and because of what the Holy Spirit confirms about our future, the Holy Spirit prompts us to claim the provision our heavenly Father wants to give to each of us as his children. What a tragedy if we settle for a golf *club* when God wants to give us a *Golf Club.*

Implications and Actions

Our text reminds us, first of all, that the source of our riches is God. Because God is our heavenly Father, we are heirs to everything God has. So often we confront the challenges of life with an eye on our own resources and understandably are overwhelmed. If we will remember that God's resources are available to us as we confront life's challenges, this will transform our perspective and inspire a new confidence in us as we live our Christian lives.

But we must also remember the scope of our riches. God has blessed us, our text affirms, "with every spiritual blessing" (1:3). Televangelists often promise that God will bless us with every material blessing. If we have enough faith, some of them promise, God will make us healthy, wealthy, and wise. Paul promised something even better. He promised that God will make us adequate for each task before us, that God will be with us as we face those tasks, and that God will bring us eventually to be with him for all eternity. If we will remember that God's blessings are spiritual in nature, this will protect us from false expectations and will keep us properly focused as we live our Christian lives.

GOD'S ELECTION

Much debate ensues among Christians about the idea of God's election. Paul raised this issue with his claim that God "chose us in him before the creation of the world" (Eph. 1:4).

How are we to understand this difficult idea? If we focus on the phrase "before the creation of the world" we might be tempted to take the position that God's election of us is strictly arbitrary, that we have no choice in the matter. That is, God has already decided that some of us are in and some of us are out.

On the other hand, if we focus on the phrase "in him" we will reach a different conclusion. The New Testament makes it clear that we have a choice about whether we will be *in Christ*.

Perhaps we can understand this somewhat complicated concept like this. God decided before the creation of the world that all those who choose to be "in Christ" will be a part of God's elect.

NOT LIVING BENEATH OUR PRIVILEGES

What can we do to make sure we do not live beneath our privileges?

- We need to remember who we are. We are God's children, heirs to all the riches of God (see Romans 8:16).

- We need to remember whose we are. We belong to the God who is able to do more than we can even ask or even think (see Eph. 3:20).

- We need to remember what God has provided for us. Paul's list in our text only scratches the surface of the things God has provided for those who love him (see 1 Corinthians 2:9).

QUESTIONS

1. Why are we so often willing to live beneath our privileges as Christians?

2. Which of the spiritual blessings cited in our text do you need to recognize more clearly in your life?

3. How does the metaphor of God as Father enrich your understanding of him?

4. What are the limitations of the metaphor of God as Father?

5. How can we remind ourselves of these provisions God makes available to us?

FOCAL TEXT
Ephesians 2:1–10

BACKGROUND
Ephesians 2:1–10

LESSON TWO

Celebrate the Difference God Makes

MAIN IDEA

We can rejoice in the difference God makes in our lives for now and forever when we trust in what God has done in Christ.

QUESTION TO EXPLORE

What difference does trusting in Christ make?

STUDY AIM

To describe the difference God makes for now and forever and to affirm or renew my reliance on what God has done in Christ

QUICK READ

The New Testament makes it clear that when we receive the gift of salvation that is available through Jesus Christ, he will make a positive difference in us from when we did not know him.

The most important life lesson for anyone to learn is how to be reconciled to God. This is an especially urgent question in our postmodernist day when many people embrace pluralism. Let me identify these two ideas: *postmodernism* and *pluralism.*

Postmodernism rejects objective truth and opts instead for an understanding of truth that is shaped by the community context or even by the single individual. The postmodern mindset tends to mix and match beliefs and practices from various religions and/or points of view. Someone has called this a "designer religion." The idea is to mix and match until you find something you like.

Religious pluralism holds that no single religion can claim absolute truth, and therefore, the different strategies presented by the different religions of the world all have validity. The result of religious pluralism is a relativism that suggests many different ways for a person to be restored to a right relationship with God.

I have been blessed and stretched by reading and learning of different points of view, but I also have some concerns about the pluralistic leanings that seem to be emerging. To me, we must keep focused on the Christian faith as we consider basic questions such as these: How can we be restored to a right relationship with God? And what difference does that right relationship make in our lives?

The most instructive answer to the previous questions is provided in the second chapter of Paul's Letter to the Ephesians. According to this passage—and this model is confirmed throughout the rest of the New Testament—salvation is *from* death (Ephesians 2:1–3) *to* life (Eph. 2:4–5) *by* grace (2:6–8) *through* faith (2:8–9) *for* good works (2:10). That paradigm answers all the basic questions concerning reconciliation with God.

EPHESIANS 2:1–10

¹As for you, you were dead in your transgressions and sins, ²in which you used to live when you followed the ways of this world and of the ruler of the kingdom of the air, the spirit who is now at work in those who are disobedient. ³All of us also lived among them at one time, gratifying the cravings of our sinful nature and following its desires and thoughts. Like the rest, we were by nature objects of wrath. ⁴But because of his great love for us, God, who is rich in mercy, ⁵made us alive with Christ even when we were dead in transgressions—it is by grace you have been saved. ⁶And God raised us up with Christ and seated us with him in the heavenly realms in Christ Jesus, ⁷in order that in the coming ages he might show the incomparable riches of his grace, expressed in his kindness to us in Christ Jesus. ⁸For it is by grace you have been saved, through faith—and this not from yourselves, it is the gift of God— ⁹not by works, so that no one can boast. ¹⁰For we are God's workmanship, created in Christ Jesus to do good works, which God prepared in advance for us to do.

From Death (2:1–3)

According to the Apostle Paul, we need to be reconciled to God because, in our current condition, we are spiritually dead. Paul affirmed that before we became Christians we were dead in our "transgressions and sins" (2:1). Paul was talking about spiritual death. A person is not *physically* dead without Christ. A person without Christ still breathes, talks, and carries on his or her life. A person is not *intellectually* dead without Christ. A person without Christ can still think and reason. A person is not *morally* dead without Christ. A person without Christ may well at times exhibit kindness and display love. Paul, though, was talking about our *spiritual* condition.

What caused this spiritual death? Paul mentioned two causal factors: "transgressions and sins." "Transgressions" refers to *deviations from the straight and narrow path.* The word means *to lose our way or to go astray.* "Sins" refers to *missing the mark* with our life. The word means *to shoot at something and miss the target.* That's what we have done with our lives. We have deviated from God's plan for our lives and have become something different from what God created us to be. The result of this deviation from God's plan is spiritual death.

Paul described this life of "transgressions and sins" as the life "in which you used to live" (2:2). When we live with "transgressions and sins," we are not living the way a Christian lives, but rather we are living the way the world lives. When we live with "transgressions and sins," we are not living under the control of Christ, but rather we are living under the control of Satan, whom Paul called the ruler of the kingdom of the air. When we live with "transgressions and sins," we are not displaying the spirit of obedience that comes from the Spirit, but rather we are displaying a spirit of disobedience that comes from the flesh.

Three forces contribute to humanity's spiritual condition: the world; the devil; and the flesh. When we sin, we allow ourselves to be controlled by the values and attitudes of the world. When we sin, we yield to the devil and let him control our lives. When we sin, we follow the inclinations of the flesh. By flesh, Paul did not mean our body but our sin nature.

Who is it that yields to the world, the devil, and the flesh, and ends up in the spiritual mortuary? Paul claimed that "all of us also lived among them at one time" (2:3). As righteous as Paul had been in his pre-Christian life, as zealous as he had been in following the law of God, Paul still included himself in the company of those who were dead in their trespasses and sins. If Paul could be included in that company, each of us is in that company too. None of us, in our own power, can break the chains of sin and escape the spiritual death that comes as a result of our sin. Jews and Gentiles alike needed to be touched by the transforming power of God in Jesus Christ and rescued from spiritual death.

To Life (2:4–5)

What then does reconciliation to God provide for those of us who were spiritually dead? What a beautiful answer Paul provided in verses 4–5. He affirmed that "God, who is rich in mercy, made us alive with Christ."

Imagine a couple receiving word that their son had been killed in combat, only to receive a telegram the next day saying that the report was a mistake. He was still alive. What great news that would be! Paul's word in verse 4 is even better news. To those of us who were spiritually dead, God has given spiritual life, a new quality of life that begins right now and lasts forever. To be reconciled to God is to be reborn into a brand new life.

When did God give us this gift of life? He gave it "when we were dead in transgressions." This spiritual transformation is nothing we achieved. Spiritual transformation is something God accomplished in us. He accomplished this transformation in our lives when we needed it most.

Paul declared that God provided this life by making us "alive with Christ." This new life that we experience as Christians was made possible because of Christ. In his virtuous life and in his vicarious sacrifice on the cross, Jesus paid the penalty for our sin. He thus made it possible for God to forgive us and restore us to a right relationship with him. Paul's statement in 2 Corinthians 5:21 is as clear an explanation of this process as we find in the New

Testament: "God made him who had no sin to be sin for us, so that in him we might become the righteousness of God."

Why does God want to reconcile us to himself and give us this new life? What is God's motive? Grace is the driving motive of God's act of reconciliation on our behalf (Eph. 2:5). Grace means that God gives us the gift of salvation, even when we don't deserve it, and God does it because of his great love for us. The love of God is almost beyond description, but the Bible makes it clear that God's love is unique, spontaneous, strong, sovereign, everlasting, and infinite. When this love is directed to us sinners, we understand it as mercy. God's mercy is as rich as God's love is great. Because of God's rich mercy and God's great love, God has given to us this new life.

By Grace and Through Faith (2:6–9)

Paul identified both the present (2:6) and the future (2:7) results of this gift of life God has provided through Christ. Right now, in the present, God has "seated us with him in the heavenly realms in Christ Jesus" (2:6). This is what we already experience right now. Just as we already have been raised up with Jesus, even so we are already seated with him in the heavenly places. Our names are already inscribed in heaven's register. Our interests are already being promoted there. The blessings of heaven are already descending on us. Right now, we are already enjoying the power and the position of being children of God.

But our passage tells us more. Some day, in the future, God will "show the incomparable riches of his grace" (2:7). This phrase, the "incomparable riches of his grace" includes blessings that we cannot even conceptualize right now. When Christ returns to consummate God's plan, we will experience these things. To those in Paul's day and in our day who are dead in trespasses and sins, this is exceedingly good news.

So how can we experience this present and future blessing? Paul answered that question with two key words: *grace* and *faith*. We are saved "by grace." This is God's part in the transaction. Grace has been described as *God's riches at Christ's expense*. Grace is the *unmerited favor of God*. The word "grace" describes God's willingness to love us when we were unlovely and to offer to us the gift of life. We are saved "through faith." This is our part in the transaction. Faith is a process that involves both the mind and the will. Faith means to believe with the mind that this gift of life is available through Christ. Faith also means to decide with the will that we want this gift and are willing to let Christ take control of our lives.

To make sure we understand that faith is our response to what God has already done rather than something that we merely do, Paul added two phrases. He added "and this not from yourselves" in verse 8 and "not by works" in verse 9. Grace comes first, and then faith responds to it. Grace is what God does. Faith is our response to what God has done. We are saved *by* grace and *through* faith.

For Good Works (2:10)

When we respond to God's grace with faith and experience the reconciliation with him that provides new life for us, both our actions and our relationships will be changed. According to verse 10, instead of doing the evil works of sin, we will begin to do the good works of faith. Our actions will change. Paul referred to us as "God's workmanship, created in Christ Jesus to do good works."

We are God's workmanship—God's creation. In other words, God reconciled us to himself so that we might be a living demonstration to the world of his power and his purpose. We demonstrate God's power and God's purpose by doing good works. Jesus expressed it like this in Matthew 5:16: "Let your light shine before men, that they may see your good deeds and praise your Father in heaven." We are reconciled *by* grace. We are reconciled *through* faith. We are reconciled *for* good works. That is the biblical pattern of how a person can be restored to a right relationship with God. We must not let anyone convince us to abandon that biblical model.

Implications and Actions

Our text offers us both a word of assurance and a word of warning. The assuring word is that God can and will transform our lives with the touch of his grace. We do not have to be a part of a select group in society. We do not have to attain a certain level of success among our peers. We do not have to demonstrate an extraordinary level of goodness. God's grace is available to every person on the same basis—faith. And faith is something that every person can have.

On the other hand, our text also offers a word of warning. Our text warns those who believe that they can somehow earn their salvation, either by their good works or by their goodness. Too, our text warns those who believe that many pathways lead us to God. The exclusiveness of the New Testament is reflected in this passage. Let us remember, too, that Jesus said, "I am the way and the truth and the life. No one comes to the Father except through me" (John 14:6).

SAVED FOR GOOD WORKS: THE SOCIAL GOSPEL MOVEMENT

Baptists have led the battle against salvation *by* good works. Baptists have also led the battle for salvation *for* good works. Some Baptists who led the battle for salvation *for* good works were a part of what came to be known as the Social Gospel movement.

The Social Gospel movement was a Protestant Christian intellectual movement in the late nineteenth century and early twentieth century. The movement applied Christian principles to social problems, especially poverty, inequality, liquor, crime, racial tensions, slums, poor schools, and the danger of war. One of the leaders was Walter Rauschenbusch (1861–1918), a Baptist. To him the kingdom of God was not a matter of getting individuals to heaven but of transforming the life on earth into the harmony of heaven.

Most church leaders did not see a connection between these issues and their ministries, and so they did nothing to address the suffering. In contrast, Rauschenbusch felt a Christian's duty was to act with love by trying to improve social conditions. He highlighted the final dimension of the paradigm presented in our text: we are saved *for* good works.

CASE STUDY

Some new neighbors invited a couple in our church to attend their worship service with them. Their worship service happened to be at a Buddhist temple. Our members agreed to go with them. Then, in the car coming back home, the Buddhist couple asked our members to come

to their house some night and discuss how Christianity was
different from Buddhism. The couple in our church asked
for advice on what to say to this Buddhist couple. What
would you have told them?

QUESTIONS

1. Why is pluralism a popular alternative today? Why
   do people find it appealing?

2. Why does *salvation by works* continue to appeal to
   many people?

3. How does today's text apply to the question of how a person can be reconciled to God?

4. Can you think of any other New Testament passages that echo or support the model for reconciliation presented in today's text?

5. How can we maintain the New Testament distinction between being saved *by* good works and being saved *for* good works? How do we sometimes blur the distinction?

LESSON THREE
Cherish All in the Family

MAIN IDEA

In Christ, God makes it possible for people to live together in cooperative, peaceful unity.

QUESTION TO EXPLORE

Why have we—Baptists, Christians, humanity—failed so badly in realizing the cooperative, peaceful unity God offers in Christ, and what can we do about it?

STUDY AIM

To describe the aspects of the unity God offers in Christ and identify ways I can realize that unity today

QUICK READ

In Jesus Christ, God brings all people together in a unity that breaks down the barriers of race, gender, and social standing that so often divide people.

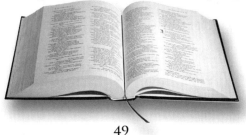

Can people really live together in cooperative, peaceful unity? Between the Jews and the Gentiles of the ancient world a wide chasm existed, a barrier that could not be crossed. Intense rivalry, even hatred, existed between these two groups. But the basic message of our text is that Jesus took these two groups who had been estranged and at war with each other and brought them together as one. Do we dare to believe that Jesus can still do this in our world today? How?

EPHESIANS 2:11–22

[11]Therefore, remember that formerly you who are Gentiles by birth and called "uncircumcised" by those who call themselves "the circumcision" (that done in the body by the hands of men)—[12]remember that at that time you were separate from Christ, excluded from citizenship in Israel and foreigners to the covenants of the promise, without hope and without God in the world. [13]But now in Christ Jesus you who once were far away have been brought near through the blood of Christ.

[14]For he himself is our peace, who has made the two one and has destroyed the barrier, the dividing wall of hostility, [15] by abolishing in his flesh the law with its commandments and regulations. His purpose was to create in himself one new man out of the two, thus making peace, [16]and in this one body to reconcile both of them to God through the

cross, by which he put to death their hostility. **17**He came and preached peace to you who were far away and peace to those who were near. **18**For through him we both have access to the Father by one Spirit.

19Consequently, you are no longer foreigners and aliens, but fellow citizens with God's people and members of God's household, **20**built on the foundation of the apostles and prophets, with Christ Jesus himself as the chief cornerstone. **21**In him the whole building is joined together and rises to become a holy temple in the Lord. **22**And in him you too are being built together to become a dwelling in which God lives by his Spirit.

The Rift (2:11–12)

Note that our text opens with the word "therefore." "Therefore" is a connective word that points back to the preceding verses and connects the thought expressed there with the thought expressed in the following verses. In the preceding verses, Paul explained that those who had been estranged from God and dead in their trespasses and sins had been brought back together with God and had been made alive in Christ Jesus. Christ broke down the barriers that existed between God and humanity and established peace between a holy God and sinful humanity.

As Jesus broke down the barriers between God and humanity and created peace between them, even so

Jesus wanted to break down the barriers between Jew and Gentile and create peace between them. Paul distinguished between the Gentiles and the Jews by calling the Gentiles "uncircumcised" and the Jews "the circumcision." Circumcision was a mark of the covenant God made with Israel. To bear circumcision on the body indicated a connection with God's chosen people. The Gentiles did not have that mark on them because they were not participants in God's covenant.

Since the Gentiles were not a part of God's covenant family, the Gentiles lacked some things. Gentiles were "excluded from citizenship in Israel." To Israel God had given his law, his special protection, and his prophecies. The Gentiles had been excluded from all of that before they came to know Christ. They did not have the benefits of citizenship in God's kingdom.

In addition, Gentiles were "foreigners to the covenants of the promise." Throughout the Old Testament period, God made covenants with his people. Actually, each of these manifestations was simply a reaffirmation of the initial covenant that God made with Abraham. A covenant is an agreement between two parties in which each has a responsibility and each makes certain promises to the other. To be a part of God's covenant is to receive God's promises. Unfortunately, the Gentiles had been excluded from these promises before they came to know Christ.

Further, Gentiles were "without hope." Hope is not based on our own strength and our own ability but is based on God's promises to us. Hope is based on the knowledge of God's promises and the confidence that God will make good on those promises. Before the Gentiles came to know Christ, they had no hope.

Finally, Gentiles were "without God in the world." The Gentiles had gods. The pagan world of Paul's day worshiped a multitude of gods. But the people of that day were without the one true God. They did not know the true God and therefore did not experience the peace, power, and purity available only through him.

The Reconciliation (2:13–16)

Because of the things the Gentiles lacked, they stood apart from the Jews. Throughout the Bible, terminology of distance was commonly used to distinguish between Jews and Gentiles. Those who were a part of the covenant with Israel were "near," but those who were not a part of the covenant with Israel were "far away" (see Isaiah 57:19; Acts 2:39). However, Jesus changed that.

Now, in Christ Jesus, those who formerly were far off have been brought near. In the past, Jews were nearby because the blood of Abraham flowed in their veins. Now, Paul explained, the ones who were nearby were those for whom Jesus had shed his blood. It was not the blood in their veins but the blood shed for them on the cross that determined whether they were nearby or far away. Jews as well as Gentiles could be "far away" if they rejected Christ. Gentiles as well as Jews could be "near" if they received Christ.

Since the determining factor in a person's life was no longer the person's blood line but his or her acceptance or rejection of Christ, "the dividing wall of hostility" between the Jews and the Gentiles has been destroyed. Previously, these two groups had been divided.

The barrier between these two peoples was formally symbolized by two things. First, a wall that separated the court of the Gentiles from the temple proper symbolized their division. No foreigner could cross over the barricade that surrounded the sanctuary and enclosure. The law and its requirements also separated the Gentiles from the Jews.

Jesus merged these two groups into one new unit (2:15). Two words in the Greek can be translated "new": *neos*, which means *new in point of time*; and *kainos*, which *means a new thing that did not exist before*. Paul here used the word *kainos* to communicate that Jesus brought together the Jews and the Gentiles and produced one new kind of person.

Jesus brought Jew and Gentile together "by abolishing in his flesh the law with its commandments and regulations." When Jesus Christ died on the cross for our sins, he removed the judgment of the law and the enmity that it caused. All are now in one group, for Jew and Gentile, male and female, have all been redeemed through the cross and brought into the family of God.

Therefore, there was no longer any difference between Jew and Gentile. The difference was between those who were in Christ and those who were not in Christ.

The Result (2:17–22)

Jesus' sacrificial work on the cross produced two things: "peace" (2:17); and "access" (2:18). "Peace" is the inner assurance that all is right between humanity and God. Jesus himself was their peace (2:14); he established peace (2:15); and he preached peace (2:17). Jesus' entire life and mission was a mission of peace. "Access" is the freedom to approach God because of the confidence that they had found favor with him. The Greek word translated "access" is *prosagoge*. This word was used in a number of ways in the ancient world. The word was used for bringing people into the presence of God so they could be consecrated to his service; for introducing a speaker or an ambassador into a national assembly; and for introducing a person to royalty. All three ideas are probably included in Paul's usage of the word in our text. Jesus provided the unparalleled privilege of coming into the presence of the God who created and rules the world. All who believe in Christ, both Jew and Gentile, were brought together through this shared peace and common access to God.

Because of the unification of both Jews and Gentiles in Christ, Paul could assure the Gentiles that "you are no

longer foreigners and aliens" (2:19). "Foreigners" trans-
lates the Greek word *xenoi*. The word means *someone
from another place*. In the ancient world, the foreigner
was always regarded with suspicion and dislike. "Alien"
is from the word *paroiko*, a word that identifies a resident
alien, a person who lived in the city but never became a
naturalized citizen. That's what the Gentiles were before
Christ came: foreigners and aliens. Through Christ, the
Gentiles' status changed.

Paul presented three images to describe this new status
of Gentiles. First of all, Paul assured the Gentiles that they
were now "fellow citizens" with the Jews. Paul used a *kingdom* image here in announcing that the Gentiles could be
"fellow citizens" in God's kingdom (2:19). This word, "fellow
citizens," represents equality in every way. First, the *terms
of admission* to the kingdom of God were the same for the
Gentile as well as the Jew. A person becomes a part of the
kingdom of God by grace through faith, and nothing more.
Too, the *standing* in the kingdom of God was the same for
the Gentile as well as the Jew. The church was not divided
into first-class Christians and second-class Christians. All
Christians are in the same class. Further, the *privileges*
extended to those in the kingdom of God were the same for
both Gentile and Jew. Some people in the kingdom did not
have more privileges than others. Both Gentiles and Jews
were equally a part of God's kingdom.

Paul next used a more intimate term to describe the
new status of the Gentiles. He asserted that they were also

"members of God's household" (2:19). The New Testament not only talks about the kingdom of God but also about the family of God. *Kingdom of God* pictures individuals who are willing to relate to each other. *Family of God* pictures individuals who are related to each other by blood. God was the father of the Gentiles as well as the Jews. This meant that Jews and Gentiles were brothers and sisters in the same family. A family was a more intimate unit than a nation. To be fellow citizens with someone else expressed at least some level of commonality and some common ambitions. To be brothers and sisters took that relationship to a deeper level of intimacy.

Paul called up a third image in verse 20. He spoke of the church as a building in which both Gentiles and Jews were the building blocks. The foundation of this building was "the apostles and prophets, with Christ Jesus himself as the chief cornerstone." The word *apostle* meant *one who is sent under the authority of another.* The term became a technical term to identify the Twelve who were the first ones chosen to follow Jesus. Paul probably had the technical meaning of the term "apostles" in mind here. As the first followers of Jesus, the apostles were foundational in the building of the church.

When Paul mentioned prophets, we immediately think about the Old Testament prophets like Elijah, Elisha, Jeremiah, and Isaiah. However, Paul was probably not referring to the Old Testament prophets. We conclude that for several reasons. First, notice the order. Paul mentioned the apostles first and then the prophets. He would probably have spoken of the prophets first if he had the Old Testament characters in mind, for they came chronologically before the apostles. Second, notice the use of the word "prophets." In Ephesians 4:8–11, the prophets are mentioned immediately after the apostles. These "prophets" were gifted by the ascended Lord and thus must have been someone in the New Testament era. Third, notice the reference in Ephesians 3:5. There again, "apostles and prophets" appear in that order, and the reference clearly excludes the prophets of the old covenant.

So what did Paul have in mind when he mentioned the prophets? The prophets of the New Testament were those who spoke forth the word of God. The foundation of the church was not only the apostles, those believers who first demonstrated the faith to follow Jesus, but also the prophets, those who faithfully proclaimed God's word.

These two—apostles and prophets—were foundational only in a secondary sense. Jesus is the primary foundation, and that is why Paul referred to him as the cornerstone. Jesus held the strategic spot in the building of the church, for he is the cornerstone. But believers were the living stones with which Jesus built his church (2:21). Paul assured the Gentiles in the closing verse that they were not excluded. They, too, were a part of God's grand work of building his church.

Implications and Actions

The church introduced some new things into the world. First, the church introduced into the world a new kind of unity. All of us experience a unity based on outward realities like our nationality, appearance, similar personalities, or lifestyles. In the church, we experience a unity that goes beyond all of those external realities, a unity based on the internal reality of our connection with Jesus Christ.

The church also introduced into the world a new kind of equality. Everything related to the church can be approached and experienced with equality. The qualifications for becoming a part of the church are the same for every person. The responsibility of faithful obedience is the same for every person. The privileges that are ours as Christians are the same for every person.

Finally, the church introduced into the world a new kind of intimacy. We know our family more intimately than we do others outside our family. The church is family. We who belong to the church are family. We have the privilege of sharing our lives with each other in a way we don't with anyone else.

COVENANT

"Covenant" is the word used to describe God's special relationship with the Hebrew people in the Old Testament.

A covenant is an agreement made between two parties. God entered into this kind of relationship with the Hebrew people. In covenant, God made certain promises to them and demanded certain obligations from them so he could fulfill his purpose and intention for humanity.

Israel, however, often became confused about God's purpose and intention. They thought the purpose of God's covenant was to bless Israel. From the beginning of the covenant idea in the Old Testament, God's purpose was to use Israel to bless the world. For example, when God inaugurated his covenant with Abraham, God not only promised to bless Abraham and his people (Genesis 12:2), but he also promised to bless all the peoples on earth through him (Gen. 12:3). In his announcement that both Gentiles and Jews were included in God's new work of redemption, Paul was simply acknowledging that God had fulfilled through the church his original intention.

HOW CAN WE FLESH OUT
THE TRUTH OF THIS LESSON?

- Claim the access to God made available to us through Jesus Christ.

- Accept others who profess faith in Christ, even if they display differences in their customs and rituals.

- Combat the forces that erect barriers to participation in God's kingdom.

- Contest those who divide believers into different classes of Christians.

QUESTIONS

1. What barriers separate us from other people?

2. What can we do to break down these barriers?

3. What are some ways in which your church demonstrates the unity described by Paul in our text?

4. Which image do you find most helpful in describing the church—the kingdom, the family, or the building?

5. Which of the images in question 4 will relate most effectively to people in today's postmodern world?

FOCAL TEXT
Ephesians 3:14–21

BACKGROUND
Ephesians 3:1–21

LESSON FOUR

Open Yourself to All God Has for You

MAIN IDEA

We need to open ourselves to God's strength and allow Christ and his love to dwell in our hearts.

QUESTION TO EXPLORE

Do you ever yearn for greater spiritual strength and nearness to Christ?

STUDY AIM

To evaluate the extent to which I truly am open to greater spiritual strength and nearness to Christ and consider ways for opening myself to all God has for me

QUICK READ

Paul interceded on behalf of the Christians at Ephesus, asking God to strengthen and deepen their faith so they could experience the full richness of the Christian life.

One of the most precious privileges of the Christian is the privilege of prayer. I suspect, however, that we do not understand or experience the full dimensions of prayer. We are good at personal *petitions*, that is, prayers in which we ask God for something. However, we often neglect other aspects of prayer, such as *praise*. How much time do we spend in our prayer life just praising God for who God is? That is a major emphasis in the Book of Psalms, which is the prayer book of the Old Testament. *Thanksgiving* is another element of prayer we may practice at certain times of the year, for example, during the Thanksgiving season. But how much time do we spend in thanksgiving at other times of the year? How about *confession*? Confession is a vital part of prayer, but how much time do we spend confessing our specific sins to the Lord and seeking the Lord's forgiveness? Yet another element of prayer that we often neglect is *intercession*, praying for others. How much time do we spend each day praying specifically for the needs of others?

Paul excelled at all dimensions of prayer. Thanksgiving was a central theme of his prayer life. As reflected in his writings, he regularly expressed his gratitude to God for others who touched and shaped his life. Paul also excelled at intercession. He always had someone on his heart, and his passion for intercession pulsates throughout his writings. Our text provides one of the clearest examples of Paul's emphasis on intercession. Let's see what we can learn from his example.

EPHESIANS 3:14–21

14 For this reason I kneel before the Father, **15** from whom his whole family in heaven and on earth derives its name. **16** I pray that out of his glorious riches he may strengthen you with power through his Spirit in your inner being, **17** so that Christ may dwell in your hearts through faith. And I pray that you, being rooted and established in love, **18** may have power, together with all the saints, to grasp how wide and long and high and deep is the love of Christ, **19** and to know this love that surpasses knowledge—that you may be filled to the measure of all the fullness of God.

20 Now to him who is able to do immeasurably more than all we ask or imagine, according to his power that is at work within us, **21** to him be glory in the church and in Christ Jesus throughout all generations, for ever and ever! Amen.

Paul's Posture (3:14–15)

As Paul interceded on behalf of his Christian friends in Ephesus, he knelt before the Father. The Bible does not prescribe one certain posture for prayer. We can pray while standing up (Genesis 18:22), sitting down (1 Chronicles 17:16), and lying prostrate on the ground (Matthew 26:39). We can also pray kneeling, as Paul did in this instance.

The posture of kneeling to pray is seen often in the Bible. In 2 Chronicles 6:12, the Bible says that in the service for the dedication of the temple, Solomon "knelt down before the whole assembly of Israel and spread out his hands toward heaven." About Daniel, the Bible says, "Now when Daniel learned that the decree had been published, he went home to his upstairs room where the windows opened toward Jerusalem. Three times a day he got down on his knees and prayed, giving thanks to his God, just as he had done before" (Daniel 6:10). In the same way, Paul knelt when he interceded for the Ephesians. We see why in verse 15.

Paul described God as the one "from whom his whole family in heaven and on earth derives its name." Paul built on the point he made in the preceding chapters. God had established a new entity made up of Jews and Gentiles. To describe this new entity, Paul focused here on the image of the family. Like a human family that takes the name of the father, this new spiritual family takes the name of its heavenly Father. We Christians get our name from him.

Because we are the family of God and God is our Father, we respect God for who he is. That's why Paul knelt when he came into God's presence in this act of prayer. Because we are the family of God and God is our Father, we can also trust God to supply every need. That's why Paul confidently came before his heavenly Father with his prayer of intercession that unfolded in the following verses. Paul prayed for four things for the Ephesians, and they are all interrelated. He prayed for strength (Eph. 3:16), for depth (3:17a), for comprehension (3:17b–19a), and for fullness (3:19b).

Paul's Prayer (3:16–19)

Paul prayed first for strength for his fellow Christians in Ephesus (3:16). He specifically asked God to strengthen them in their "inner being." The inner being is the center from which our feelings and thoughts emanate. The writer of Proverbs tells us that out of the heart, or the inner being, are the issues of life (Proverbs 4:23). That is where we need to be strengthened, in our inner being, where all of our decisions are made. Our outer being—the physical—is gradually deteriorating each day. This was true of the Ephesians as it is of us today. So Paul prayed that their inner being—the spiritual—would be renewed and strengthened daily.

This strengthening takes place "through his Spirit." The real power by which we live our lives is not human power. It is spiritual power. We do not face our challenges, carry out our assignments, or handle our problems in our own strength. We face these challenges, carry out these assignments, and handle these problems through the strength of the Holy Spirit dwelling in us. Therefore, Paul prayed that the Ephesian Christians might experience the spiritual power that God made available to them.

In his intercession for the Ephesian believers, Paul also prayed for depth (Eph. 3:17a). He prayed that Christ would "dwell" in their hearts. The word for "dwell" is a Greek word that refers to *a permanent residence*. As Christians, Jesus already dwelt in their hearts. However, Paul asked that Jesus would be at home in their hearts, that he would be a permanent resident.

Several times each year, my wife Jan and I go to Kansas City to stay with Jan's family. But this visit is just a temporary stay. We sleep in someone else's bed. We live out of the suitcase. We stay for a few days and never feel completely at home because that is not our permanent residence. But at the end of the trip, when we get back to our home, put our clothes away, and go to sleep in our own bed, we feel at home.

Our personal experience sheds light on Paul's intercession for the Ephesian Christians. Paul prayed that Jesus would not just pass through their lives but that he would instead be a permanent resident. How can that happen? Paul explained that it happens "through faith." As the Holy Spirit strengthens the inner person, faith in Christ deepens, and as faith deepens, the person feels that Christ makes his home in his or her heart.

Paul interceded for a third thing for the Ephesian Christians. He prayed that they would come to a deeper understanding of the quality of God's love in Christ Jesus. Paul was not just praying for mental understanding but for a comprehension "that surpasses knowledge." Paul had in mind not just *head* knowledge but also *heart* knowledge. He did not just want the Ephesians to *comprehend* the love of God—that is, understand it. He wanted them to *apprehend* the love of God—that is, to take it into their lives.

How could the Ephesians apprehend this love and take it into their lives? Paul mentioned two qualifiers. First, they must apprehend God's love "together with all the saints." When lives are opened to other believers and experiences are shared with them, both their understanding and our understanding will expand. Second, they must be "rooted and established in love." Paul mixed his metaphors here, bringing together the idea of a tree with its roots and a building with its foundation. In both cases the meaning is the same. For a tree to be stable, its root system must be deep enough and extensive enough to support the spread of its branches. For a building to be stable, its foundation must be strong enough and deep enough to support the height of the structure. The lesson from these metaphors translated into the life experience of those to whom Paul wrote in this way: Only as they extended the roots of their lives deeply into the love of God and only as they built their lives on the foundation of God's love would they be able to comprehend the full dimensions of God's love.

Finally, Paul prayed for fullness. He wanted the Ephesian Christians to "be filled to the measure of all the fullness of God" (Eph. 3:19b). Did Paul mean he wanted the Ephesians to become like God, to have all the attributes of God? No. Instead, he wanted them to experience all of the attributes of God they had the capacity to experience. In other words, he prayed that the Ephesian believers would realize their potential—that they would use their gifts to the fullest, that they would extend their influence to the fullest, that they would expand their understanding to the fullest, and that they would develop their love to the fullest. He prayed that they would experience all of the fullness they had the capacity to experience.

Paul's Praise (3:20–21)

Do all the things for which Paul interceded seem possible? If it were up to Paul or the Ephesians, the answer would be *no*. But Paul recognized the *God factor* in his life and in the lives of the Ephesians. With God, anything is possible, for God is completely sufficient. Contemplation of the splendid adequacy of God elicited from Paul a doxology of praise. Paul piled word upon word to sketch a picture of God's sufficiency.

Paul affirmed that God is able to do everything we ask him to do (3:20). That in itself is a fantastic promise, but it is only the platform on which Paul painted this verbal portrait of God. God is not only able to do the things we ask him to do, but God is also able to do the things we dare not ask him to do, things we only imagine. All the dreams that have ever passed through our minds, all the things we have thought of accomplishing for God in our wildest imagination—God is also able to do those things. Paul expanded further this picture of God's adequacy by adding that God is not only able to do those things that we ask about and think about, but God is also able "to do immeasurably more." Paul formed a unique compound word out of three Greek words. This compound literally means *to go beyond going beyond all things in an inexhaustible way.* Paul painted the picture of an absolutely adequate God.

Paul then connected this lofty portrait of the adequacy of God with the power that was already at work in this world. The same power with which God created the world, the same power with which God brought Jesus back from the grave, and the same power with which God brought about our redemption is the same power at work within us. It is sufficient to do much more than we could ever conceive in our minds or ask God with our mouths to do. Could the Ephesians experience the strength, depth, apprehension, and fullness of which Paul spoke? Or, on a more personal level, can we experience these things today? Yes, we can, because of the superabundance of God's resources.

Implications and Actions

What does all of this mean for us today? Our text reminds us, first of all, that the Christian life offers more than we have yet experienced. You may have been a Christian for many years and have experienced a quantity of spiritual power and a quality of love that is truly remarkable. Yet, no matter what you have seen or done or felt or experienced as a Christian up to this point, God has more in store for you.

In addition, our text reminds us that we have a greater power available to us than human power. If everything in our lives that we have accomplished for Christ can be explained by our own gifts or intellect or ability or power, then we have not yet gone far enough in our Christian walk.

Further, our text reminds us that the Christian life is not just about *me*. We will begin to apprehend the depth and breadth of God's love only as we relate to other Christians in the church. That's why our involvement in the life of the church is crucial.

INTERCESSION

What is *intercession*? When used as a description of prayer, intercession means an arranged meeting with God to talk about someone else.

For what should we pray as we intercede with God for someone? An answer can be found in the example of Moses. Moses prayed for the people of Israel to make atonement for their sins (Exodus 32:30). The word *atonement* means *to cover* and is related to an act of grace by which offenses were covered so that fellowship could be restored between an offender and the one offended. That is, Moses' intercession was for the purpose of restoring the Israelites to fellowship with God. So restoring one to fellowship with God should always be the purpose of intercession.

Intercession means praying for someone for the purpose of securing God's grace for that individual so that fellowship with God and usefulness for God will be established or maintained.

WHY INTERCEDE FOR OTHERS?

Why should we be involved in prayers of intercession?

- Because of the command of Scripture
- Because of the example of great Christians of the past
- Because of our connection with other believers
- Because of the need in the lives of others
- Because of the effectiveness of prayer

QUESTIONS

1. Can you name an aspect of prayer that you have neglected? In which of the elements of prayer are you weakest? strongest?

2. For whom do you intercede in prayer on a regular basis?

3. When you intercede for others, do you pray that they may have an easier life, or do you pray for them to have a deeper faith?

4. Can you identify some biblical characters known because they interceded for others?

5. Why is our association with other Christians important for developing our own Christian life?

LESSON FIVE

Grow Up into Christ—Together

MAIN IDEA

We are to lead a life worthy of our Christian calling by growing up into Christ, together.

QUESTION TO EXPLORE

Have you grown any lately as a Christian?

STUDY AIM

To describe the worthy life Paul begged Christians to live and identify specific ways I will practice what Paul preached

QUICK READ

Paul offered the Ephesian church, which brought together Gentile and Jewish Christians, clear instruction and careful nurture to help the two groups overcome a history of mistrust and animosity.

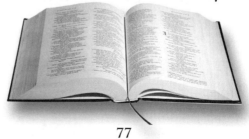

The small group had met for several weeks. Members were getting to know one another and building a level of trust, as groups are designed to do. They had been carefully exploring critical doctrines of their faith, looking at God's truth from many directions. They had discussed the work of God in Christ, defining such terms as grace, faith, and salvation. Finally, one perceptive participant raised the question, "We've been doing a lot of talking about God. Why don't we get serious about how to live for God in the world where we spend our lives?"

In a sense, helping new Christians get serious about how to live for God is what Paul began to do in Ephesians 4. Having set forth in the earlier portions of Ephesians some meaningful insights about God's nature and God's will for his people, Paul next explored what that meant for the life of God's people.

Remember that the recipients of this letter were likely hearing these lofty and revolutionary truths for the first time and thus needed practical instruction for applying them to their daily lives. How would they put these ideals into action as they followed the way of Christ? Beginning in chapter 4, Paul offered guidance and instruction in a variety of applications as he encouraged his hearers to live a life worthy of the great gift of God's grace in Christ.

EPHESIANS 4:1–16

¹I therefore, the prisoner in the Lord, beg you to lead a life worthy of the calling to which you have been called, ²with all humility and gentleness, with patience, bearing with one another in love, ³making every effort to maintain the unity of the Spirit in the bond of peace. ⁴There is one body and one Spirit, just as you were called to the one hope of your calling, ⁵one Lord, one faith, one baptism, ⁶one God and Father of all, who is above all and through all and in all.

⁷But each of us was given grace according to the measure of Christ's gift. ⁸Therefore it is said,

"When he ascended on high he made captivity itself a captive;

he gave gifts to his people."

⁹(When it says, "He ascended," what does it mean but that he had also descended into the lower parts of the earth? ¹⁰He who descended is the same one who ascended far above all the heavens, so that he might fill all things.) ¹¹The gifts he gave were that some would be apostles, some prophets, some evangelists, some pastors and teachers, ¹²to equip the saints for the work of ministry, for building up the body of Christ, ¹³until all of us come to the unity of the faith and of the knowledge of the Son of God, to maturity, to the measure of the full stature of Christ. ¹⁴We must no longer be children, tossed to and fro and blown about by every wind of doctrine, by people's trickery, by their craftiness in deceitful scheming. ¹⁵But

speaking the truth in love, we must grow up in every way into him who is the head, into Christ, **16**from whom the whole body, joined and knit together by every ligament with which it is equipped, as each part is working properly, promotes the body's growth in building itself up in love.

Worthy of the Calling (4:1–6)

The text begins with a challenge that grew out of their "calling," or *vocation*. Paul had a deep conviction that all who follow Christ do so in response to God's action (Ephesians 1:11–14). No doubt Paul would always remember his Damascus road experience in which the risen Christ confronted him even though he was actively working against God's purposes (Acts 9:1–6). Paul would always feel that before he had chosen Christ, God had chosen him. Paul's appeal here was that those who had been called must devote themselves to living a life that honors and respects their calling.

In Ephesians 2:1–22, Paul emphasized to Gentile Christians that God had acted in Christ to include them in the circle of his love. Jew and Gentile were brought together as one people through the gifts of God's love and grace in Christ. In truth, they had been called to a new life. This calling was not their own doing and was in no sense the result of their striving. It was God's gift of grace, so eloquently stated in Ephesians 2:8–9, "For by grace you have been saved through faith, and this is not your own doing; it is the gift of God—not the result of works, so that no one may boast." If God has so generously given life, it becomes the Christian's responsibility to live a life that honors that gift through obedience, growth, and sincerity.

The goal of such worthy living is "unity of the Spirit in the bond of peace" (Eph. 4:3), a task best approached with "all humility and gentleness, with patience, bearing with one another in love" (4:2). We must keep in mind the deep enmity that had built up between Jew and Gentile by the first century. Remember the amazement of a woman at the well when Jesus, having dared to go through Samaria, asked her for water? "'How is it that you, a Jew, ask a drink of me, a woman of Samaria?' (Jews do not share things in common with Samaritans.)" (John 4:9).

Note the words used in Ephesians 4:2 to describe the spirit of those who live in a manner worthy of their calling, building the kind of unity within the church that God seeks. "Humility" refers to that quality of honestly seeing our own condition and thus laying aside the grounds for pride. Recently I saw a sign that declared, "Much humiliation leads to a little humility." If we honestly see ourselves as sinners saved only by God's grace, then there is no room for putting down another who also is a sinner saved only by God's grace.

"Gentleness" grows out of a respect for others by one who has discovered how a gracious God has gently reached out to us. How rich are the examples in Scripture of Jesus' gentle treatment of those to whom he ministered, often people with flawed character.

"Patience" describes the opposite of the short-temperedness and intolerance of this world. Instead, those who seek to embody the worthy life practice a perseverance with others that will not be stopped. Even in the face of insult and injury, the person who has learned the spirit of Christ continues to work for the good of others.

The fourth word of this powerful passage, "love," enables the other three. "Love" is the quality that so cherishes the worth of every other person that it will not stop seeking that which is best for another. This trait of Christian character was so different from other ideas of love that the New Testament writers chose a little-used Greek word, *agape*, to represent it. Different from the love of friends, the love of a husband and wife, or even the love of family members for one another, this *agape* love is the spirit God has shown humanity in the self-giving love of Christ.

As these great qualities are put into action in a church setting, there results a "peace" that is the bond of true fellowship. When pride, inconsiderate treatment of others, and harsh attitudes have been replaced by humility, gentleness, patience, and love, something marvelous happens to a group of God's people. The resulting unity underscores how Paul could envision Jewish and Gentile believers living in harmony and effective service in their churches. There was not a Jewish church and a Gentile church. There was one body of believers. There was only one Lord, one faith, one baptism—not separate ones for different groups of people—just as there is only one God and Father of all.

This unity in the churches was a demonstration of the truth Paul also described in his Letter to the Galatians. There we read, "There is no longer Jew or Greek, there is no longer slave or free, there is no longer male and female; for all of you are one in Christ Jesus. And if you belong to Christ, then you are Abraham's offspring, heirs according to the promise" (Galatians 2:28–29).

What a powerful witness it was to see Jew and Gentile, once strangers and enemies, now bound together in humble love of one another as a family of believers. This unity was not a dull sameness in which everyone was alike. It was a living, growing, energized body of believers with all the varied gifts and abilities of its diverse members, linked together through the calling of God. Would that we might see more of that spirit in our churches today!

The Gifts that Assist Us Toward Maturity (4:7–12)

This section of the epistle moves from the character of the members to the gifts that God has given to assist in living out that character. Paul quoted from Psalm 68:9 but with one significant difference. The psalm speaks of the practice of an ancient king who has been victorious in a battle. The king had captives, and he led them up the hill to the city and forced them to march through its streets in humiliation, demanding gifts or ransom from a defeated people. Here Paul shows the spirit of God who finds us captive to our sin and disobedience, defeats our sin through Christ, and now *gives* gifts to us, his people.

The victorious Christ gives to his people that which is essential for their new life. This Son of God who "descended" into the realm of human experience, even in the realm of the dead, has now "ascended" in victory, having accomplished what God intended for his people (Eph. 4:9). He has given gifts to assist us in the process of maturity. God's goal for God's people is a unity of spirit and life, and God has offered help for the process.

Paul mentioned four examples of gifted leaders sent to assist God's people on their journey. He began with "apostles," those who had seen Jesus and witnessed his words and wonders as well as the resurrection. These were the voices respected for their first-hand experience with the Lord. Paul always considered himself to be an apostle, not as one of those who followed Jesus during his earthly ministry, but as one who met the risen Lord in a miracle of grace.

Second in this list are "prophets." These should not be thought of primarily as predictors of the future but more like preachers. They spoke of the consequences of disobedience as they called for faithfulness to the will of God.

"Evangelists" were travelers throughout the regions to which Paul was writing. Think of them as missionaries who knew the message of the life of Jesus and who interpreted this to people who likely had never heard of him.

Finally Paul described "pastors and teachers." Both terms likely describe two functions of one person in a church. Pastors and teachers were persons whose task was to nurture new converts. Those new believers largely came out of religious traditions with little knowledge of either the Jewish or the new Christian faith.

The primary role for these four types of leaders is to build up the church and strengthen it for its mission in the world. Note carefully that these leaders were sent "to equip the saints for the work of ministry, for building up the body of Christ" (Eph. 4:12). Their purpose related again to God's great vision in Christ of a church united across cultural and ethnic differences, growing toward a mature fellowship of service and witness.

The Goal of Christian Growth Together in the Church (4:13–16)

Paul summarized this section by returning to the theme of unity in the fellowship. The divine plan is to build "up the body of Christ." This is accomplished when Christians mature in their relationships to the Lord and one another. This is not a unity of enforced sameness, but of people united in a growing devotion to Christ. Many of our divisive encounters in this life grow out of childish self-centeredness. Paul urged his friends in Christ to "grow up" (4:15).

The church is at its noblest when it remembers and lives out the metaphor of the church as the "body of Christ." When Christ is the head and every member assumes his or her role, depending on gifts, talents, abilities, and opportunities, the church's mission can be fulfilled.

Implications and Actions

We are living in an age that tests the goal of unity in the churches. We are tempted to follow a path of self-interest and individualism that plays down our need for others. Churches would do well to emphasize in a fresh way the essential need we have for fellowship, encouragement, and nurture in a congregation united in the love and grace of God.

Some of my greatest moments in many decades of ministry have occurred when I have seen land owners and tenants; supervisors and factory workers; management and labor; men, women, and children; and white, black, Asian, and Hispanic people sit together in worship before the one true God. Things that our culture has allowed to become barriers separating people dissolve.

Bridges are built when we live out the implications of God's gifts of grace to all. Make no mistake; these bridges often are built only after struggle and resistance. Deeply ingrained customs and prejudices do not go away without prayerful application of God's kind of love. The witness of a unity of spirit among God's people, however, is a powerful testimony to the power of the gospel.

THE BAPTIST WORLD ALLIANCE

In 1904, Baptist leaders in the United States and Great Britain agreed on the wisdom of a gathering of Baptists from around the world to demonstrate the unity experienced under the Lordship of Christ. This vision resulted in the first Baptist World Congress in London in 1905. The Baptist World Alliance grew from that small beginning and now includes more than 200 Baptist conventions and unions.

Those who attend gatherings of this worldwide fellowship of Baptists are often amazed at the diversity of people who come, crossing borders and boundaries of culture, race, and nationality, to affirm their faith in one Lord. Language, dress, and style of worship may be quite different, but when voices and hearts are together singing, praying, and proclaiming the love of God we have learned in Christ, there is a unity of Spirit that is thrilling. The Baptist World Alliance continues to exemplify a practical expression of the ideal our text describes of a people united by the gracious love of God.[1]

HOW TO BUILD UP THE UNITY OF ALL BELIEVERS

- Determine to follow God's word in your relationships with all people.

- Spend time each day identifying those from whom you feel separated, examining why you may feel this separation.

- Prayerfully seek specific ways to reach out to people with whom you feel this separation.

- Develop a small group of other believers who are willing to explore ways to be more inclusive of people our society has alienated.

QUESTIONS

1. Which of these qualities—"humility," "gentleness," "patience," and "bearing with one another in love"— presents the biggest challenge in your Christian growth? How can you mature in that quality?

2. The ideas of "Gentile" and "Jew" may not represent the issues of a divided church in our day and time. What categories of people have we allowed to separate us in our churches today?

3. Where or in what way do you feel most prepared to fulfill your personal ministry?

4. In what ways have you been blessed by ministries of love and grace in your own personal experience? Identify some person(s) to whom you or your class could extend a loving ministry.

NOTES —————————————————————————————

1 For additional information on the Baptist World Alliance, see www.bwanet.org.

FOCAL TEXT
Ephesians 4:17—5:2, 11–16

BACKGROUND
Ephesians 4:17—5:20

LESSON SIX

Follow the Directions

MAIN IDEA

Saved only by God's grace through faith, Christians are to learn Christ and live accordingly.

QUESTION TO EXPLORE

How can we apply Christian teachings on behavior in our permissive society without becoming pharisaical?

STUDY AIM

To identify the teachings in this passage that are most challenging for me to apply and decide to do it anyway

QUICK READ

Paul challenged new converts who came from pagan lifestyles to allow the spirit and power of the risen Christ to transform their lives into living witnesses.

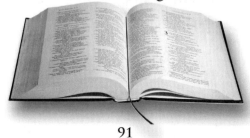

Some years ago, I was privileged to lead a small group to an East African country to teach pastors and church leaders about stewardship. While I knew that stewardship was about much more than money, one of the great lessons I learned on that trip was how people of a different culture and background approached the subject. They had little in the way of material possessions or money to give through their churches. Stewardship for these Christians was more an understanding of their new way of life. In this new understanding, their primary gift to God was a transformed life to be used in the service of their Lord. Many of the people who came to our sessions demonstrated a powerful witness of dedication and character.

The text for this lesson speaks of people coming out of a pagan culture who needed to understand what a Christian life should look like. Although they had been saved by God's grace, they needed to learn a way of life that demonstrated their new relationship to God.

Most of us would agree that the Christian faith is an ethical religion, meaning that following Christ has an impact on the behavior of a believer. Interpreting the life and ministry of Jesus and applying it to current issues is a task for every generation of followers of Christ. Doing so presents contemporary preachers and teachers with two challenges.

First, caution is in order lest we turn the Christian message into a set of legalistic requirements necessary to earn God's favor. We are tempted to seek detailed rules and regulations to cover every issue of life. Such was the failure of Pharisaical religion in the first century.

A second challenge is not to reduce our understanding of the ethical nature of Christian living and the miracle of God's grace to simplistic bumper sticker statements or clever billboard slogans. We do a disservice to the life-changing power of the gospel when we reduce it to mere moralisms. The complexity of our world demands a spirit of humble seeking for the best way to honor the gift of new life that God has offered us in Christ. It is a daily search as we go about our life at home, at work, or in the broader civic arena.

The author of these challenging verses continued to appeal to the new believers to leave old ways of living and turn to a new and dynamic relationship with God through Christ. Paul was, however, aware of the danger of a legalistic religion resting merely on the good works of human beings.

EPHESIANS 4:17—5:2, 11–16

17Now this I affirm and insist on in the Lord: you must no longer live as the Gentiles live, in the futility of their minds. **18** They are darkened in their understanding, alienated from the life of God because of their ignorance and hardness of heart. **19**They have lost all sensitivity and have abandoned themselves to licentiousness, greedy to practice every kind of impurity. ²⁰That is not the way you learned Christ! ²¹For surely you have heard about him and were taught in him, as truth is in Jesus. ²²You were taught to put away your former way of life, your old self, corrupt and deluded by its lusts, ²³and to be renewed in the spirit of your minds, ²⁴ and to clothe yourselves with the new self, created according to the likeness of God in true righteousness and holiness.

²⁵So then, putting away falsehood, let all of us speak the truth to our neighbors, for we are members of one another. ²⁶Be angry but do not sin; do not let the sun go down on your anger, ²⁷and do not make room for the devil. ²⁸Thieves must give up stealing; rather let them labor and work honestly with their own hands, so as to have something to share with the needy. ²⁹Let no evil talk come out of your mouths, but only what is useful for building up, as there is need, so that your words may give grace to those who hear. ³⁰And do not grieve the Holy Spirit of God, with which you were marked with a seal for the day of redemption. ³¹Put away from you all bitterness and wrath and anger and wrangling and slander, together with all malice, ³²and be kind to one another, tenderhearted, forgiving one another, as God in Christ has forgiven you. ^{5:1}Therefore be imitators of God, as beloved children, ^{5:2}and live in love, as Christ loved us and gave himself up for us, a fragrant offering and sacrifice to God.

[11] Take no part in the unfruitful works of darkness, but instead expose them. [12]For it is shameful even to mention what such people do secretly; [13]but everything exposed by the light becomes visible, [14]for everything that becomes visible is light. Therefore it says,

"Sleeper, awake!

Rise from the dead,

and Christ will shine on you."

[15]Be careful then how you live, not as unwise people but as wise, [16]making the most of the time, because the days are evil.

Leaving the Old Way for a New Way in Christ (4:17–24)

The beginning appeal is to "no longer live as the Gentiles live" (Ephesians 4:17). The recipients of this letter have previously been labeled as "you Gentiles" (Eph. 3:1). In verse 17, "Gentiles" means more than merely those who were not Jews. We might use the term *pagan* to describe these Gentiles. Their lives and values had been shaped by traditions and religious ideas quite different from the biblical teaching. These verses continue a theme stated in Ephesians 2:12: "Remember that you were at that time without Christ, being aliens from the commonwealth of Israel, and strangers to the covenants of promise, having no hope and without God in the world."

Wrapped into these verses is a description of the old ways in which the Gentiles had lived before coming to know Christ. They were products of a world that knew nothing of Christ. The revolting picture that emerged reflected a depraved people who had lost the meaning of life as God intended it. Several vivid phrases describe their state.

They were "darkened in their understanding" (4:18), in part because of their ignorance of the truth. The word for "ignorance" in this verse is a word that typically means *ignorance caused by circumstances that might be overlooked* (Acts 17:29–30). What follows, however, indicates a "hardness of heart," which implies a conscious determination to resist any inclination to do good. The resultant alienation from godly living produced the vices that follow.

Having "lost all sensitivity" (Eph. 4:19) to the error of their sin, they openly flaunted their godlessness. Few people set out intentionally to practice godless living. At first there is resistance to the temptations, but as one engages in ungodliness, it becomes easier to repeat the error until one loses a sense of what is right.

We are reminded of the steps toward immorality described in Psalm 1:1: "Blessed is the man who does not walk in the counsel of the wicked, or stand in the way of sinners, or sit in the seat of mockers" (NIV). A person first walks by sin, then stands and listens to the logic of the skeptics, and finally joins their gathering, having lost sensitivity to the errors involved.

The progression of the pagans continues as "licentiousness," becoming *greedy to practice every kind of impurity* (Eph. 4:19). There is no list here of the specific sins the author had in mind, and such a list is not necessary. The emphasis is on the person who has lost a moral compass, no longer feeling any remorse for conduct that degrades and abuses self and others. As followers of Christ, they must leave that way behind them. Using the image of taking off an old garment that was filthy and unfit, these new disciples must clothe themselves with a new way of living that they would learn from the example of Christ.

Living in the Light (4:25—5:2)

Imitation is a word we view with some alarm. Something about artificial plants, foods, and fibers seems to rub us wrong. "Imitation" sounds like something phony, artificial, and inferior to the real thing. Yet Christians are urged to be "imitators of God" (5:1) as we live out the new life offered through Christ. Far from being called to an artificial or phony way of life, believers are called to a new and exciting discovery of all that is real and true. In these verses, new converts find guidance as they ponder the implications of the new way of life they have accepted.

It is important to remember that these words are directed to persons who have already accepted God's gracious gift of salvation in Christ. We must not forget the foundational words of a previous lesson: "For by grace you have been saved through faith, and this is not your own doing; it is the gift of God—not the result of works, so that no one may boast" (2:8–9) . Far from offering a set of rules one must keep to earn God's acceptance, the words of chapter four are given to those who are to live lives of grateful witness to what God has done. These verses offer instruction and guidance for converts who have heard the good news of God's love and now must learn to live God's way in a culture that was far from godly. Consider some of the issues mentioned here.

Believers are challenged to honesty: "putting away falsehood, let all of us speak the truth" (4:25). Most civilized people value honest talk, and we feel a sense of moral outrage when we discover that a trusted person has misled us. The text goes even further to urge us to put away double talk that doesn't communicate truth.

"Be angry but do not sin" (4:26) acknowledges a common human emotion. Paul cautioned the new believer not to allow anger to fester until it erupted in an abuse of another person. We would do well to confess our anger, deal with it, and leave it behind.

The Christian is urged to leave behind dishonest gain and engage in useful undertakings instead (4:28). Have you known people who have boasted of their honesty and wouldn't think of taking another's money or property, but who don't think twice about cheating on an expense account or hedging on taxes? These forms of stealing do not demonstrate the kind of life that reflects the spirit of our Lord.

"Let no evil talk come out of your mouths, but only what is useful for building up" (4:29) is yet another reminder of the power of words to hurt or help. This phrase may bring to mind a lesson spoken by many a caring parent who has reminded a child, "If you can't say something good about another person, don't say anything!" In a culture such as ours, with foul and obscene language so prevalent, surely believers in a holy, gracious, and loving God should reflect something better.

Finally, Paul listed a series of things that need to be put aside by those who would demonstrate honorable living. Bitterness, wrath, anger, wrangling, slander, and malice (4:31) must give way to kindness, tenderheartedness, and forgiveness (4:32), because this is the way God has dealt with us in Christ.

The instructions in this section of the text are a powerful reminder that the Christian way is not primarily about doctrines and definitions. The way of Christ is about living out God's love in the way we treat others. This way is not something one does simply in church services or class meetings. The Christian way is to produce acts of love, grace, and mercy in everyday contact with human beings who need to see God's grace in action.

The author's challenge was for his hearers to be "imitators of God," reflecting the spirit of God to the world around them. This is no mere outward copying of a few ethical behaviors, but rather doing what God did in Christ to reveal the divine nature to humanity. "Beloved children" (5:1) are to show their heavenly Father's nature as they "live in love" in the same way Jesus did, reflecting the spirit of Christ, who so freely gave his life for us.

Making the Most of the Time (5:11–16)

From the text for this lesson, the author clearly does not suggest that the converts withdraw from the world. He emphasized instead the importance of a new and different way of life for new believers who came to follow Christ out of pagan cultures and religious practices. One thinks of Jesus' metaphors of "salt" and "light" (Matthew 5:13–14), which indicate that Jesus' disciples would bear witness to the power of the gospel and make a difference in their world. The only way Christians and their churches will be heard in our world is by living a life of integrity and compassion. That was the way Jesus chose to live. The old adage is true: our actions will speak louder than our words.

In Ephesians 5:14, words from an unnamed poet are used to urge the believers to wake up and allow the light of Christ to shine through committed lives. The frequent image of light as the truth of God's revelation in Christ contrasts with the darkness of a pagan way of life.

The emphasis on living in the light of God's truth concludes with a wonderful call for each person to make "the most of the time" (5:16). None of us knows how many opportunities we will have to be salt and light. There is no time to waste in our determined following of our Lord.

Implications and Actions

For several years, I worked in a denominational position, largely involved with ministers and churches in all of their complicated and often conflicted relationships. Often the struggles within congregations grew from contentious attitudes and harsh words and left me wondering where the real Christians were. Anger over old issues that should have been resolved and laid to rest was allowed to grow and fracture the congregation. People demanded that others follow their lead or join their side. They were determined to win an argument at all costs. Mean-spirited words gave rise to broken relationships that were never repaired. The wisdom of this section of Ephesians could guide all of us in our congregations when inevitable conflicts arise.

One of the lessons I learned in those years was that a person earns the right to lead. Leadership is not a role that can be demanded, conferred by vote, or given by the laying on of hands. Leaders earn the right to lead as they walk with others through the everyday experiences of life. The same is true for the believer's witness in the world. Our most effective challenge to the calloused and insensitive ways of our world is to live out the spirit of our Lord. He met people where they were, loved each of them, and gave his life for all.

IMITATORS OF GOD

The Greek word *mimesis* (the source of our English word *mimic*), translated in Ephesians 5:1 as "imitators," would have been quite familiar to first-century hearers. The word was associated with the common method of teaching in many fields of endeavor, particularly oratory. The method involved observing and repeating the actions of an exemplary person. When one wanted to be trained to be an orator, the person seeking to learn would find a master orator and carefully imitate every move and technique.

In the same way, if one would live out the kind of life God intends for God's people, the best method is to fix one's eyes on Christ. Observing the way Jesus treated others becomes the way Jesus' followers should pattern their lives.

LIVING UP TO CHRISTIAN STANDARDS

An adult who has been attending your church has shown interest in becoming a Christian. In conversation with this person she confesses, "I would like to become a Christian, but I'm not sure I could live up to the standards I hear in our pastor's sermons." What counsel could you offer?

QUESTIONS

1. The text mentions the images of "darkness" and "light." What are some of the things that those images bring to mind?

2. How can Christians encourage godly living and Christian work without diminishing the truth of salvation that comes by God's grace?

3. How can a Christian achieve the goal expressed in the challenge, "Do not let the sun go down on your anger" (Eph. 4:26)?

4. In what ways could your class help one another to accomplish the goal of growth in the new way of life this passage describes?

FOCAL TEXT
Ephesians 5:21—6:4

BACKGROUND
Ephesians 5:21—6:9

LESSON SEVEN

Be Christian in Family Relationships

MAIN IDEA

All relationships in the home are to be ordered by reverence for Christ.

QUESTION TO EXPLORE

How does Christian faith affect relationships in the family—or does it?

STUDY AIM

To describe differences that would result if I ordered all my family relationships by reverence for Christ

QUICK READ

Family relationships are deeply spiritual in nature, and in this passage we find reminders of the basic qualities of love and respect that Christ reveals for these family ties.

For many people, family reunions are special moments of celebration. Watching strong families get together at seasonal events, designated reunions, or other gatherings is a joy. To hear the laughter, reminiscences, and good-natured banter among people who genuinely care for one another is an inspiration. Even in the most difficult times of grief and sorrow, to see families pull together and find hope and strength is a powerful testimony.

Where do such family ties come from? In spite of what we sometimes hear from politicians about "family values," careful observation shows us that strong family life is built on much more than party planks. Our text in this lesson brings to light the true biblical foundation for Christian families. In a word, it is the spirit of Christ applied to every aspect of family life that brings the greatest strength.

EPHESIANS 5:21—6:4

21Be subject to one another out of reverence for Christ.

22Wives, be subject to your husbands as you are to the Lord. 23For the husband is the head of the wife just as Christ is the head of the church, the body of which he is the Savior. 24Just as the church is subject to Christ, so also wives ought to be, in everything, to their husbands.

25Husbands, love your wives, just as Christ loved the church and gave himself up for her, 26in order to make her holy by cleansing her with the washing of water by the word, [27]so as to present the church to himself in splendor, without a spot or wrinkle or anything of the kind—yes, so that she may be holy and without blemish. [28]In the same way, husbands should love their wives as they do their own bodies. He who loves his wife loves himself. [29]For no one ever hates his own body, but he nourishes and tenderly cares for it, just as Christ does for the church, [30]because we are members of his body. [31]"For this reason a man will leave his father and mother and be joined to his wife, and the two will become one flesh." [32]This is a great mystery, and I am applying it to Christ and the church. [33]Each of you, however, should love his wife as himself, and a wife should respect her husband.

[6:1]Children, obey your parents in the Lord, for this is right. [2]"Honor your father and mother"—this is the first commandment with a promise: [3]"so that it may be well with you and you may live long on the earth."

[4]And, fathers, do not provoke your children to anger, but bring them up in the discipline and instruction of the Lord.

First-Century Households

The counsel offered in this lesson's text is directed at roles common to households of the first century. As with the interpretation of any portion of Scripture, one must explore the setting in which the participants were involved.

Among other things, these new Christians of Asia Minor were living in the midst of a culture that held family life to be important. Philosophers and wise teachers had enunciated clear values for a well-ordered household. In that culture, the legal system declared the husband to be the head of the family, with power and property rights over family members. Christians, having been introduced to the understanding that all stand equally in Christ, had to find appropriate ways to express that equality within the first-century household setting.

A further factor these first-century Christians had to deal with was the belief by many non-Christians that Christians were somehow a threat to stable community life. Paul wished to counter this belief by demonstrating that believers in Christ also shared a commitment to strong, stable, and orderly households.

The background passage for this lesson includes directives for slaves' obedience to their earthly masters and masters' treatment of their slaves (Ephesians 6:5–9). While the presence of household slaves would have been common in the first century, we have learned through the centuries the evils of slavery. Christians would not try to reinstate this practice, even though Paul does not condemn it here. In the same light, there are now, and always have been, many variations of family life. Not all homes have a father or a mother present. Not everyone is married, and all married couples do not have children. Interpreting these words of guidance for today's households requires careful and thoughtful reflection on how the spirit of these words can be applied to a very different cultural setting.

The principles described in these verses are important for all societies since healthy and holy relationships make for more stable communities. Indeed, these words about family relationships could well apply to all relationships. This section follows the earlier verses of chapter 5 about conduct in the church. The church is to become the visible presence of Christ in the world, shaping lives and shedding light about life as God intends it to be lived.

The Foundation of All Christian Relationships (5:21)

This verse bridges the preceding description of the life of the Christian in a community of faith and the family relationships that follow. Sober, reverent worship and expressing thanks to God for his gifts of grace are qualities described in 5:1–20 for believers in the church. Verse 21 lays down the basis for this life together as believers being "subject to one another out of reverence for Christ." It is not just a few who are to practice this submission, but all who enter into a commitment to Christ and his church and who live together as a household of faith.

This spirit of humility in relationships is often stated in the writings of Paul. He offered this advice in Romans

12:3 about building up the body of Christ: "I say to everyone among you not to think of yourself more highly than
you ought." Humility is truly the foundation on which the
people of God must build their conduct with respect to
others. Pride and exclusiveness do not reflect a way that
honors the limitless love of God in Christ.

Note also that Paul appealed to them to be subject to
one another "out of reverence to Christ." To understand
Paul's words about family relationships requires some
reflection on his ideas about Christ and the church. We
would not think that being subject to Christ as head of the
church involves abuse in any way. To accept Christ as Lord
is to enter into a relationship of love and gratitude, of grace
and celebration. This relationship enhances and builds up
the believer and never denigrates another person.

Christians being subject to one another out of reverence for Christ is the foundation on which the following
words about family life are built. To miss the spirit of
Jesus in his compassionate and redemptive bond with his
people could lead to a domineering attitude that is foreign
to the spirit of Christian homes.

Husbands and Wives (5:21–33)

In recent years, there has been much discussion among
people of faith about the relationship of husbands and
wives, with the emphasis being on who is in charge. On

the one hand, there are those who point to this passage of Ephesians as indicating husbands have absolute control over household decisions with wives simply backing them up. Others insist that Scripture gives wives equality with husbands in a more democratically governed marriage. They would point to such passages as Galatians 3:28, which states, "There is no longer Jew or Greek, there is no longer slave or free, there is no longer male and female; for all of you are one in Christ Jesus." We are not likely to find a definitive answer to this issue in the text before us, but we can see the spirit in which any healthy relationship of husband and wife must be formed.

Building on the concept of mutual submission (5:21), observe the specific advice offered to wives and husbands. We can assume from the context that both are believers and seeking guidance about how being Christian impacts marital relationships. The advice offered is inseparably tied to the commitment of two people to Christ and to each other, and out of their connection to the church of which they are more than spectators. The relationship of wives and husbands in the church will be a witness to their faith in Christ as head of the church and Lord of their lives.

Wives are instructed to be subject to their husbands with the same spirit of surrender that they have made to Christ (5:22–24). The submission they have made to Christ is not one of fear and defeat, but one of joyous discovery of a loving Lord. So, a wife who finds in her husband a soul mate who has her best interest at heart will gladly listen to his guidance. The Greek word for *submission* used here does not imply an inferiority of personhood but rather describes subordination to one who is worthy of respect. Like godly love, such an attitude reflects a spirit that puts another first.

Lest husbands be tempted to turn their wives' submission into an autocratic rule over them, they were admonished to love their wives with the same kind of love and reverence they have expressed to Christ (Eph. 5:25–30). This appeal is very important for Christians, given that in first-century culture, marriages were not necessarily built on love. Men took wives to bear children, to guarantee heirs, and to carry on the husband's name. That Christian marriage was to be built on a loving relationship placed heavy responsibility on the husband coming out of cultural values that were quite different. The perfect example for this kind of love is seen in Christ who "loved the church and gave himself up for her" (5:25).

Many cities and towns have hidden away somewhere a shelter for abused family members. It is offered as a place of refuge for those who have suffered spousal abuse. To see battered and bruised wives in hospital emergency rooms and shelters is to be reminded of the pain that comes when Christian love is not the guiding principle of marriage.

Verse 28 urges husbands to "love their wives as they do their own bodies." In the Greek culture of that period, some people considered the body as sinful and urged an ascetic existence in which bodily desires were repressed.

For Paul, this position was erroneous. Using the image of the church as the body of Christ, he upheld human relationships in the church and, more specifically, in marriage. The Christian life is to be lived in the world as an example of the new life that faith brings.

Christian couples must decide on a pattern that best honors their marriage relationship as husband and wife. Whatever conclusion they reach, they can be certain that the kind of selfless, generous, and uplifting love exhibited by Christ for his church should be the guiding principle. Nothing in that kind of love permits abuse, insensitivity, or boorish behavior. Rather the partnership of two Christians who are committed to each other in love is a relationship of respect and honor of one for the other.

Thinking back over many years of ministry, my mind turns to so many wonderful couples. I think of those who have suffered the stresses of the loss of a child or of vocational moves, illnesses, and disappointments. Yet they have found a peace and contentment made strong through shared experiences. Their relationships have been strengthened and enriched by the abundant love they have shown to each other with patience and persistence.

Children in the Christian Home (6:1–4)

The imperative offered to children to obey their parents is rooted in the authority of Old Testament Scripture as the "first commandment with a promise" (Exodus 20:12; Deuteronomy 5:16). Ephesians 6:1 says that this obedience is "in the Lord." The child's obedience is not merely to please earthly parents or to simply get along with them. This obedience is done out of a sense of responsibility to God who wills it as right.

Children are obedient, not for the convenience of parents, but to build the kind of family life in which the young learn from the experience and example of loving parents.

Fathers are given special emphasis since they were earlier described as head of the household. As in the relationship of husbands and wives, the father's leadership is not intended simply to grant power and authority to men but to underline the necessity for Christian fathers to demonstrate the spirit of Christ in their homes. Children in that culture were considered to be the property of their fathers. The fate of a child at birth was in the hands of a father who could decree that the infant be left to die. That the child's future was largely determined by the decisions of the father makes Paul's words more forceful.

Caution is prescribed for fathers lest their manner of dealing with their children be too harsh. No doubt Paul had seen the results of cruel and thoughtless treatment of children, including fearing that such treatment could keep them from coming to a faith of their own in Christ as the loving Lord.

Implications and Actions

The quality of Christian love is the foundation on which godly household relationships are built. Christian homes are built in an environment of love and grace in which all family members have opportunity to find faith and see it mature in powerful witness.

Few would deny that family life is under great strain in American culture. Hectic schedules, economic pressures, and secular values push families to the limits of endurance. There is a tremendous need for the application of warm and loving relationships within these pressures. Family life affects everyone in our society.

Christianity begins in the community of faith as persons gladly submit to the lordship of Christ, but the impact goes much further. Changed lives take that faith home and live it in family relationships. Those changed lives reach out to build responsible neighborhoods and healthy communities.

Reading passages such as this lesson's text can bring a sense of guilt to us as we realize times in which we have failed to live up to the standard of love toward spouse, children, or our own parents. Where loving, supportive relationships have been formed, there is an environment for healing and restoration of family ties.

LOVE (*AGAPE*)

The Greek language has a variety of words with rich and subtle meanings. Three of these words—*philos, eros,* and *agape*—are typically translated by the one English word *love*. The kind of love that Paul urged as the basis of husband-wife relationships is unique in its application in Scripture. Where *philos* is the love of one's friend, and *eros* has to do with sensual love, *agape* is used exclusively as God's kind of love. It is generous to the extreme, seeking always to give to another and to work for another's good. It is beautifully described in the words of 1 Corinthians 13.

When Paul urged husbands to love their wives, it was this godly kind of love that was required. Such love is unselfish, patient, kind, and forgiving. It is the kind of love God has extended to us in Christ.

HELP FOR A SINGLE MOTHER

A single mother with two teen-aged children shares with you her concern about her oldest daughter's behavior. The mother describes her daughter's angry outbursts and lack of respect for her mother. What advice would you offer to this mother whose household does not fit the pattern described in the text for this lesson?

QUESTIONS

1. Think of the varieties of family types that you see in your church or community. Which of these types do you think were present in the first century? In what ways do the principles of love and respect apply in each form of family life you have identified?

2. In what way do the verses of today's lesson apply to the unmarried or couples who have no children? Does this excuse them from concerns about families or how children are treated in American families?

3. How do you feel family life affects the quality of life in communities?

4. Think of ways in which your life has been impacted by the family relationships that have been part of your life. Can you share some of these with your class?

The Letter to the Philippians

So how can we live with faithfulness and joy? The second source in this study for answering this question is the Letter to the Philippians.

Philippi was a city in Macedonia (the general area of northern Greece and the nation of Macedonia today). Paul had founded the church there a few years before (see Acts 16:11–40).

The immediate circumstance in which Paul was writing was imprisonment (Philippians 1:12–14). In spite of this, however, Paul's Letter to the Philippians is upbeat rather than somber. A sense of joy, contentment, generosity, and well-being permeates the letter, overflowing from Paul's life. The lessons in this unit from Philippians will provide us further guidance in living with faithfulness and joy.[1]

UNIT TWO. PHILIPPIANS

NOTES ─────────────────────────────

1. Unless otherwise indicated, all Scripture quotations in the
   Study Guide lessons on Philippians are from the New American
   Standard Bible (1995 edition).

FOCAL TEXT
Philippians 1:12–14, 19–26

BACKGROUND
Philippians 1:1–26

LESSON EIGHT

See Life from an Eternal Perspective

MAIN IDEA

Living from an eternal perspective means exalting and proclaiming Christ, trusting him to care for us in whatever circumstances we face.

QUESTION TO EXPLORE

What best gives meaning and perspective to life?

STUDY AIM

To describe what Paul's focus on Christ did for him and what it will do for us

QUICK READ

In prison, Paul said that regardless of the outcome of his trial, his life was totally devoted to Christ. Paul lived life from an eternal perspective.

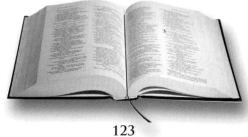

A close friend's uncle was a walking miracle and testimony of God's power. Owen Leech heard the devastating word, *lymphoma.* He was an athlete and coach, and he and his wife Dot had a six-month-old son and five-year-old daughter. Yet cancer is no respecter of persons.

As Owen began his chemotherapy treatments, he was given six months to live. By the sheer mercies of our Lord, he continued living, witnessing, and even praising the Lord although he was constantly under the threat of death. A gifted musician, he also sang in various churches. People in and beyond his immediate circle of friends and acquaintances heard of his unshakeable faith.

After years of successful struggle by Owen with the cancer, a tumor in his neck began to overtake him, paralyzing his vocal cords. Within a year he was unable to sing or even speak. Owen's fellow church members and admirers wondered whether he would fade from the scene into solitude. On the contrary, in the following Sundays he returned to church with little regard to his failing health. Every week he sat with his church family. Although not able to preach or sing, he participated in the service, smiling brightly.

Owen knew that God had provided his every need. Even better, God had provided a testimony through him for countless hurting people that Christ's gospel is greater even than cancer and the finality of death. Long ago, he had been given six months to live, and yet God granted him more than twenty-seven additional years to live. At his death, Owen left an incredible testimony for our Lord amidst dire circumstances. He knew the joy of the Lord.

This joy of the Lord often is pointed out as one of Paul's main themes in his Letter to the Philippians. He wrote this letter around A.D. 62, when he received information from Epaphroditus about the church in Philippi (Philippians 2:30; 4:18). Paul wrote to encourage the believers in that church, which was mostly Gentile. The Christian community in Philippi appears to have been suffering for their faith. Paul told them of his own circumstances and encouraged them to become more like Christ. He shared that the key to life is having an eternal perspective, with the joy of the Lord as an abiding quality.

Even when internal struggles hit the Philippians, Paul wrote, they could preserve unity through humility and love. Further, he pointed out that the ultimate joy of the Lord lies in unity of purpose, a partnership in sharing the gospel. If the Philippians were faced with attempts to stop their spreading of the gospel, they could now recall Paul's exhortation to rejoice in the Lord and to realize that "to live is Christ and to die is gain" (Phil. 1:21).[1]

PHILIPPIANS 1:12–14, 19–26

[12]Now I want you to know, brethren, that my circumstances have turned out for the greater progress of the gospel, [13]so that my imprisonment in the cause of Christ has become

well known throughout the whole praetorian guard and to everyone else, **14**and that most of the brethren, trusting in the Lord because of my imprisonment, have far more courage to speak the word of God without fear.

• • • • • • • • • • • • • • • • • • • •

19For I know that this will turn out for my deliverance through your prayers and the provision of the Spirit of Jesus Christ, **20**according to my earnest expectation and hope, that I will not be put to shame in anything, but that with all boldness, Christ will even now, as always, be exalted in my body, whether by life or by death. **21**For to me, to live is Christ and to die is gain. **22**But if I am to live on in the flesh, this will mean fruitful labor for me; and I do not know which to choose. **23**But I am hard-pressed from both directions, having the desire to depart and be with Christ, for that is very much better; **24**yet to remain on in the flesh is more necessary for your sake. **25**Convinced of this, I know that I will remain and continue with you all for your progress and joy in the faith, **26**so that your proud confidence in me may abound in Christ Jesus through my coming to you again.

The Incredible Expansion of the Gospel During Paul's Prison Stay (1:12–14)

Paul noted his imprisonment in verse 13 by saying, "My imprisonment in the cause of Christ has become well known throughout the whole praetorian guard and to everyone else." He shared that an incredible expansion of the gospel had taken place as a result of people hearing about his circumstances (1:12). Even the whole praetorian guard, soldiers placed closest in proximity to Roman leadership, had heard the gospel through personal contact (1:13). In addition, Paul had received reports that most of the Christians were encouraged by Paul's imprisonment to spread the gospel with increased confidence (1:14). This mission report would have encouraged the Philippian Christians.

Paul's situation as a prisoner in Rome entailed a long story. Perhaps picture him sitting in his prison, praising God, when suddenly a guard asked, *What on earth brings a religious man like you to this prison?*

Paul might have replied,

I'll give you the short version. It all began in Jerusalem several years ago when I was falsely accused of bringing a Greek man into the Jewish temple, which would have defiled it. As a result, a mob of Jews beat me, desiring to kill me, until, thank God, several Roman soldiers arrived. These soldiers took me, flogged me according to their custom, and placed me in chains at their barracks. They were terrified when they learned that I am a Roman citizen. They had mistakenly punished a Roman citizen without a trial.

With the temple leaders in Jerusalem in an uproar, Commander Claudius could not settle the case and sent me to Governor Felix in Caesarea (Acts 22—23). Felix dragged the case out for two years, hoping to get a bribe out of me until his successor Portius Festus next got stuck with me. Festus only decided that King Agrippa would make the decision.

Agrippa heard the whole story of my arrest, even the glorious message of Christ's death and resurrection, just as Christ had prophesied (Luke 21:12). He sympathized with my case and would have released me except I had appealed to Caesar (Acts 25:11-12; 26:32). Thus off to Rome I sailed. After enduring many hardships, including a shipwreck and a snake bite, I arrived here safely and have been in prison ever since (Acts 27—28). Ironically, I always desired to come to Rome to share Christ. Who could have imagined that God would use such an adventure to bring me here!

The Inevitable Exaltation of Christ Whatever Happens to Paul (1:19–21)

In verses 15–18 Paul provided an example of the unstoppable expansion of Christ's gospel "whether in pretense or in truth" (Phil. 1:18). Impure teachers had preached "in pretense" but sincere preachers "in truth." However, Paul rejoiced that the gospel was spreading regardless of the source.

In the remaining passage (1:19–26), Paul wrote with confidence that he knew two items for certain that were of great comfort to him. In verses 19 and 25, Paul used the Greek word *oida*, which means *to know for certain*.[2] In verse 19, when using this word, he returned to the discussion concerning his imprisonment. He exclaimed, "I know [for certain] that this will turn out for my deliverance" (bracketed words added for explanation). Notice the word "this" in verse 19. One has to back up a bit in the passage to see that "this" refers to the whole situation of his imprisonment. Paul thus stated confidently that he would find deliverance from his imprisonment.

Consider the phrase, "this will turn out for my deliverance" (1:19). In the Greek, this phrase is identical to the words Job uttered in Job 13:16, according to the Septuagint (the Greek translation of the Old Testament that was widely read in Paul's day). Both Paul and the Philippian Christians would have been familiar with this version of Scripture since Greek was their basic tongue. Thus Paul appears to identify with Job's experiences of suffering and ultimate vindication. Just as Job ultimately was delivered from his situation, so he, Paul, believed that since this was written in Scripture he too could count on such deliverance from the Lord. Therefore, his confident use of "I know" had its source in our Old Testament Scriptures.

Paul quoted Job's words with confidence in the promise of the Lord that in the end he would be vindicated. The gospel would still be preached to a world in need.

In verses 20 and 21 Paul inferred that he was uncertain as to the *how* of his personal deliverance—whether it would be on this side of eternity or the other side. He said, "Christ will even now, as always, be exalted in my body, *whether by life or by death*" (Phil. 1:20, italics added for emphasis). Regardless of the outcome of his imprisonment, of one thing Paul was certain: the inevitable exaltation of Christ.

The Inspiring Effort of Paul to Place Christ in Full Focus (1:21–26)

One might wonder how Paul expected to prevail in the face of death. Perhaps, as was common in Greco-Roman society, Paul was tired of living his life under harsh circumstances. However, he said, "For to me, to live is Christ and to die is gain" (1:21). In the Greek, Paul emphasized the word translated "to me" by placing it at the beginning of the sentence. By this placement of the word, Paul expressed his inmost perspective. In Paul's view, life consisted of maintaining an unbroken focus on Christ and on making Christ known to all the world.

In the experience of those around Paul in Rome, all that mattered in life was this earthly existence. To a pagan person death was "gain" only in the sense that the earthly struggle was finished.[3] In contrast to this dreadful view of death, Paul proclaimed that both in life and after physical death, he had and would have fellowship with Christ. Death was not merely "gain" in the sense that his struggles on earth had ceased. On the contrary, he gained a better life at death! Not only would Paul's earthly struggles be but a memory, but also his fellowship with Christ would be perfect for all eternity. Death for Paul was only a gateway through which to walk into the presence of his Christ.

In verses 22–26 Paul addressed what continued life in the flesh (life on earth) would mean to him. He concluded that life could mean only fruit for Christ from his labors. Remember that Paul had said "For to me, *to live is Christ* and die is gain" (1:21, italics added for emphasis). In the verses following, Paul noted that staying alive would result in "fruitful labor" for Christ and thus was equally desirable.

Paul again used the Greek word *oida*—"I know"—in verse 25 (as in 1:19), saying, "I know that I will remain and continue with you." He desired to comfort the Philippian Christians with the certainty that God would allow him to continue assisting them as long as he was needed. He anticipated much joy in a possible reuniting with the Philippians but assured them that all future boasting toward him would be even greater in reference to their Lord Jesus Christ.

Implications and Actions

Life lived from an eternal perspective, even in times of hardship, focuses beyond present circumstances on opportunities for the gospel of Christ to expand throughout the world. This consistent perspective on matters of eternal value deepens our relationship with Christ.

Are we able to say emphatically with Paul, "For to me to live is Christ and to die is gain"? Do we focus too doggedly on life's present circumstances? Or are we able to see beyond life's present circumstances and proclaim the gospel? We must make Christ our main focus so we can live life from an eternal perspective. Are you ready to live beyond your circumstances?

GRECO-ROMAN VIEWS OF DEATH

A range of views existed among the pagans of Paul's day concerning death and afterlife. The ancient Greek philosopher Plato (428–348 B.C.) wrote that death " . . . is a good thing. For the state of death is one of two things: either it is virtually nothingness, so that the dead has no consciousness of anything, or it is, as people say, a change and migration of the soul from this to another place."[4] Interestingly, he also wrote, "And if it is unconsciousness, like a sleep in which the sleeper does not even dream, death would be a wonderful *gain*" (italics added for emphasis).[5]

The gain of which Plato spoke was the mere absence of conscious awareness.

Plutarch (about 46–120 A.D.), a Greek historian and contemporary of Paul, pictured death in this way: "The soul, being eternal, after death is like a caged bird that has been released. If it has been a long time in the body, and has become tame by many affairs and long habit, the soul will immediately take another body and once again become involved in the troubles of the world."[6] Thus in the pagan view of death, the "gain" from death was no gain at all.

QUESTIONS

1. Where was Paul likely imprisoned and why?

2. Paul mentioned in verse 14 that some believers shared the word of God with far more courage due to Paul's circumstances. Why would this have been so?

3. How do you relate to Paul's magnificent statement in verse 21?

4. In what sense does your perspective on life and death differ from that of a person without Christ?

5. Can you think of a time when someone you know who was in difficult circumstances saw opportunity to share the gospel with others amidst those circumstances?

N O T E S

1. Gordon D. Fee and Douglas Stuart, *How to Read the Bible Book By Book: A Guided Tour* (Grand Rapids, Michigan: Zondervan, 2002), 353–356.

2. The Greek word *oida* conveys the idea of knowing with certainty or intuitively (used in Phil.1:16, 19, 25; 4:12, 15). Another Greek word that means *to know, ginooskoo*, indicates a sense of knowing by experience (see 1:12; 2:22; 3:10; 4:5).

3. Gerald F. Hawthorne, *Philippians*, Word Biblical Commentary, volume 43 (Waco, Texas: Word Books Publisher, 1983), 45.

4. Plato, *Apology* 40 C.

5. Plato, *Apology* 40 D.

6. Plutarch, *Consolation* 5.10.

LESSON NINE

Follow Christ's Pattern of Life

MAIN IDEA

When we truly live under the Lordship of Christ, we will follow Christ's example of humility.

QUESTION TO EXPLORE

Why is it so hard to be humble?

STUDY AIM

To contrast the humility seen in Christ's example to how human beings tend to behave and to decide on ways I will put Christ's example into practice

QUICK READ

Paul calls Christians to live lives worthy of the gospel. Such lives are marked by unity and humility. Paul points believers to the ultimate example of humility in Jesus Christ.

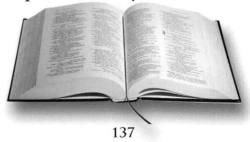

Do you ever struggle with the ideas of service and humility? Henri Nouwen did. Nouwen was a distinguished theologian and author of more than forty books on religious subjects. Educated in the Netherlands, he became a renowned professor at the University of Notre Dame, Yale University, and Harvard University. At the peak of his teaching career, this Roman Catholic scholar was a widely-known conference speaker and author and was much admired. However, although he taught about relating to God, Nouwen felt so rushed about everything in life that in spite of his achievements and his prolific writing about knowing God and relating to God, he felt his life did not fulfill its purpose.

Frustrated, Nouwen went for six months as a missionary to South America, followed by a time in France. There he spent time ministering in a home for the mentally and physically challenged. At last Nouwen felt truly nourished by a loving community. As a result, Nouwen decided to accept an invitation to become priest in residence at a place called Daybreak in Toronto, Canada, which was similar to the community in France.[1]

As a priest, Nouwen led a simple lifestyle, which formed a stark difference from his previous way of life as an internationally-known professor, author, and speaker. For the next ten years until his death, he spent his days attending to the needs of people who often were unable to talk or walk, and who often grunted or drooled during the religious services Nouwen led for the community.

During his years in Daybreak, Nouwen formed a special friendship with one of the residents, named Adam. Nouwen personally assisted Adam in morning routines. The popular Christian writer Philip Yancey once asked Nouwen about his interaction with the people in Daybreak since so little of what Nouwen said and did as a priest would seem to make sense to them. Nouwen told Yancey that getting Adam ready took him nearly two hours each day, but that "bathing and shaving him, brushing his teeth, combing his hair, guiding his hand as he tried to eat breakfast—these simple, repetitive acts had become for him [Nouwen] almost like an hour of meditation."[2] Many people might wonder whether others were more suited to assist Adam with his morning routines. Perhaps such people believe that a theologian is better suited for important tasks, like teaching and writing, rather than spending time on such humble tasks as brushing the teeth of a mentally challenged person. "I am not giving up anything," Nouwen insisted, when asked about serving at Daybreak, "It is I, not Adam, who gets the main benefit from our friendship."[3]

In the eyes of the world, Nouwen might appear to have given up everything. However, he had found that serving was a joy. He had followed Christ's example of humility and found rest for his soul. He was part of a community in which the members humbly served one another in unity.

Serving one another in humility is especially difficult in a competitive and sometimes cruel world. Paul knew

well the challenges life posed to a Christian in Roman
society since he himself was imprisoned because of his
ministry for Christ (Philippians 1:13). Nevertheless, if
Christians were to spread the gospel, humility toward one
another was key.

In Philippians 1:27–30, Paul encouraged the believers
in Philippi to live lives worthy of the gospel. As the community of God, these believers were to exhibit virtuous
lives and display unity with one another. The members of
this community had to serve one another humbly.

Philippians 2:1–11 amplifies this emphasis. Verses 5–8
provide a succinct and profound depiction of the incarna-
tion—Christ coming to earth to dwell among people and
live a life of humility. Christians are to seek to follow in
Christ's footsteps in a life of service and humility.

PHILIPPIANS 2:1–11

¹Therefore if there is any encouragement in Christ, if
there is any consolation of love, if there is any fellowship of
the Spirit, if any affection and compassion, ²make my joy
complete by being of the same mind, maintaining the same
love, united in spirit, intent on one purpose. ³Do nothing
from selfishness or empty conceit, but with humility of mind
regard one another as more important than yourselves;
⁴do not merely look out for your own personal interests,
but also for the interests of others. ⁵Have this attitude in

yourselves which was also in Christ Jesus, **6**who, although He existed in the form of God, did not regard equality with God a thing to be grasped, **7**but emptied Himself, taking the form of a bond-servant, and being made in the likeness of men. **8**Being found in appearance as a man, He humbled Himself by becoming obedient to the point of death, even death on a cross. **9**For this reason also, God highly exalted Him, and bestowed on Him the name which is above every name, **10**so that at the name of Jesus every knee will bow, of those who are in heaven and on earth and under the earth, **11**and that every tongue will confess that Jesus Christ is Lord, to the glory of God the Father.

The Exhortation to Unity (2:1–4)

Philippians 2 opens with a transitional phrase with which Paul guides the reader masterfully from chapter 1 to chapter 2. The opening phrase in 2:1, "Therefore if," refers back to Paul's faithful suffering in chapter 1 in general and to the entire preceding paragraph—verses 27–30—in particular. Likewise, the reference in verse 2 to the believers being "of the same mind" further clarifies Paul's exhortation for the Philippian believers to stand firm in unity as worthy representatives of the gospel (Philippians 1:27).

The appeal to same-mindedness is stated in the form of four conditional statements—that is, *if-then* statements. In verse 1 these statements are prefaced by "if." In

English these conditional statements may appear vague. However, in the Greek language the manner in which these statements are phrased means that the answers to the statements are assumed to be *yes*. A free translation of verses 1–2 would be: *Therefore since I assume encouragement in Christ, consolation of love, fellowship of the Spirit, and affection and compassion, make my joy complete by being of the same mind, maintaining the same love, united in spirit, intent on one purpose.* Thus Paul encouraged the believers in Philippi to stand firm in unity because of the profound intimacy Christ provides daily.

The key for maintaining unity is four-fold. The believers must be of the same mind, maintain the same love, and be united in spirit and in purpose (Phil. 2:2). Paul wrote that his joy was completed if the believers sought unity. This mention of completing his joy declares Paul's nurturing care for his beloved church in Philippi.

Note that Paul's exhortation to be "of the same mind" (2:2) does not imply mere intellectual uniformity—everyone believing the same things about life and matters of faith. Rather, the Greek phrase Paul used for the "same mind" refers to the believers' emotions, attitudes, and will in an overall sense of loyalty to the body of Christ.[4] Likewise, the believers were to have the same attitudes of love, Christ's unconditional love.

Paul's charge to be united in spirit is expressed by a unique Greek word, *sumpsuchoi*. The word was possibly coined by Paul and can be translated *one-souled*. This word connects this section of the letter to the phrase *mia psuche* in 1:27, which likewise can be translated as *one soul*. Thus conducting oneself worthy of the gospel of Jesus Christ meant being united on the level of the inner self, mind, thoughts, feelings, heart, and being.[5] Finally, Paul emphasized that this unity includes unity of purpose (2:2). Ultimately, this unity of inward attitudes is essential for the spiritual well-being of the church.

The Philippians were to avoid actions motivated by selfish ambition or empty conceit (2:3), as was the case with those who were preaching Christ from envy and strife (1:15–17). The believers were not to boast in themselves or to seek honor for themselves. Rather, they were to act in humility, regarding others better than themselves (2:4) and to focus on contributing to the needs of others.

The Example of Christ in Humility (2:5–8)

Paul next presented Christ as the ultimate example of humility. Paul exhorted the Philippian Christians to adopt the attitude of Christ, who embodied humility (2:5). The verses that follow contain a beautiful description of the mindset of Christ.

Scholars often refer to verses 6–11 as a hymn. The origin of this hymn is much debated. Did Paul write the hymn? Was this a well-known hymn in the early Christian church? Was it an ancient song that had been

Christianized and used by Paul? Regardless of its origin, the hymn set forth the mindset the believers in Philippi ought to have at all times—the mindset of Jesus Christ.

Jesus' example of humility was illustrated by his not using the fact that he was God ("although He existed in the form of God") to his own advantage (2:6). The text clearly indicates that Christ shared the same nature with God. This means that Christ was and is God in every way. Thus Jesus, when he walked and ministered on earth, regarded others as more important than himself, just as Paul instructed the Philippians (2:3). Jesus' right to claim ultimate superiority is without question. However, he walked in obscurity.

Not only did Jesus Christ walk in obscurity, but he also humbled himself by emptying himself of the status he could have claimed as God. Instead of claiming this status as God, Jesus took on the status of a "bond-servant" by being made in the likeness of humanity (2:7). Note that this was a matter of Jesus' *status*, not of his *being*. Jesus did not cease to be God when he "emptied Himself" (2:7). Rather, Jesus "emptied Himself" of the status and honor that was his as God and took on the status of a common person.

Although the text mentions that Jesus took on the form of a "bond-servant," or slave, one does not have to think that he therefore had what we might consider to be the *appearance* of a slave. First of all, first-century slaves did not have a particular distinguishing appearance. More importantly, "bond-servant" likely is a reference to Jesus' radical servant attitude. Jesus was a person among people (2:8). His focus was to serve people. Interestingly, crucifixion in antiquity was associated with the punishment of slaves (see the small article, "The Shame of the Cross"), and Jesus was the ultimate slave or "bond-servant."

For human beings death is inevitable. However, Jesus, being fully human and fully God, was not forced to face death. Jesus voluntarily and humbly went the path of utmost humility and shame by dying on a cross (2:8), the most shameful death in the first-century Mediterranean world. In this manner of death, Jesus took on the status of a lowly and utterly despised person.

Verse 8 is not focused as much on Christ's obedience as on the nature of Christ's death, to which he voluntarily subjected himself. The message of the text is intensified at the end of verse 8 as the verse clarifies the manner of Christ's death. As if death itself was not sufficient, Christ endured "even death on a cross"! Thus the utter humility of Jesus Christ becomes clear, for Jesus voluntarily put the well-being of humanity before that of himself. Paul held up Christ's model of humility as an example for the Philippian believers.

The Exaltation of Christ by the Father (2:9–11)

In verse 9 Paul proclaimed that God "highly exalted" Jesus as a result of Jesus' voluntary humility, even in obedience to death on a cross (2:9). Jesus was given a name that was

"above every name" (2:9). One's name and one's reputa-
tion, or status, were inherently interconnected in the
first-century Mediterranean world.[6] Thus Jesus was given
the honor and status that is above everyone else's status.
Jesus went from utmost shame to utmost glory by being
exalted by the Father.

Due to this highest status, every other knee in creation
has to bow for Jesus and recognize Jesus' Lordship (2:10).
Likewise, every creature capable of giving praise has to
direct that praise to Jesus, thereby declaring Jesus Lord
(2:11) and recognizing Jesus for who he truly is—the One
who went down in humility and rose in glory. In confessing Jesus as Lord, something else is declared as well: the
glory and status of God, the Father. Only God the Father
can grant total Lordship to the Son. Thus in confessing
Jesus as Lord, we recognize also the awesome glory of
God the Father (2:11).

Implications and Actions

In Philippian 2:1–11, Paul strongly urged the Philippian
Christians to seek unity. The key to this unity was to consider other believers better than themselves and focus on
the needs of others.

Such a focus requires humility. For the ultimate example of humility one must look to the example of Jesus
Christ. Since Jesus lowered himself to the lowly status

of becoming like a human, even a servant, and died the most shameful and painful death, he can identify with us in our struggles. Even more so, if we say we are Christ's followers, we likewise are asked to follow Christ by being humble people.

We are not alone in our efforts to live humble lives. We have the example of Jesus Christ and the comfort and help of the Holy Spirit. Humble lives will lead to lives of forgiveness, lives of love and reconciliation, and lives that display the gospel of Jesus Christ.

THE SHAME OF THE CROSS

Crucifixion was used by the ancient Assyrians, Phoenicians, and Persians to punish, humiliate, and scare disobedient slaves. Thus, initially crucifixion was known as a means of punishment for slaves.[7] By the first century A.D., the Romans started to use crucifixion as capital punishment for slaves and others of low status in society in cases of robbery and rebellion.

The Romans perfected the cruel nature of crucifixion . The one crucified was hung totally naked in a public place, with bodily fluids running down the body. Once the person was dead, family members often would not claim the body, for doing so would shame the entire family. Rather, the dead were thrown into mass graves.

Crucifixion often took place on a tree. In Old Testament

times corpses sometimes were hung on trees. Any dead body hanging on a tree was considered cursed in the Old Testament (Deuteronomy 21:22–23). Thus, especially in a Jewish society, anyone associated with a crucified person bore the shame of being associated with one who had been executed as a lowly slave and left as a cursed corpse.

HUMILITY

False humility secretly seeks to be blessed in the end. True humility is content with one's gifts and purpose in the body of Christ. True humility considers others first.

QUESTIONS

1. What does it mean to you to follow the One who was shamed?

2. In what sense does Philippians 2:8 shed light on what Paul wrote in Romans 1:16a, "For I am not ashamed of the gospel. . ."?

3. Can you think of a time when humility shown by someone else brought you closer to Christ?

4. How can we be better leaders in our families and churches by being more humble? Does humility harm one's ability to be an effective leader?

5. What are five practical ways by which we could train ourselves to be more humble this coming week?

N O T E S

1. Philip Yancey, *Christianity Today* (December 9, 1996): 80.

2. Yancey, 80.

3 Yancey, 80.

4 Gerald F. Hawthorne, *Philippians*, Word Biblical Commentary, volume 43 (Waco, Texas: Word Books Publisher, 1983), 68.

5. "Psuche," 26.4. *Greek-English Lexicon of the New Testament Based on Semantic Domains*. Eds. Johannes P. Louw and Eugene A. Nida. Vols. 1 & 2 (New York: United Bible Societies, 1989).

6. Bruce J. Malina, *The New Testament World: Insights from Cultural Anthropology*, third edition, revised and expanded (Louisville, Kentucky: Westminster John Knox Press, 2001), 37.

7. Vassilios Tzaferis. "Crucifixion—The Archaeological Evidence," *Biblical Archaeology Review* (January/February 1985): 48.

CAL TEXT

pians 3:1–14

KGROUND

Philippians 3:1—4:1

LESSON TEN

Seek the Highest Goal

MAIN IDEA

Faithful and joyful Christian living means seeking the highest goal, the goal of knowing Christ fully, even becoming like him in his self-giving sufferings and death.

QUESTION TO EXPLORE

What goal in life are you seeking?

STUDY AIM

To affirm or reaffirm my life goal as being to know Christ fully

QUICK READ

Paul called the believers' attention to the false teachers in Philippi. These opponents, most likely Jewish Christians, represented values that strongly conflicted with the exceedingly great value of knowing Christ intimately.

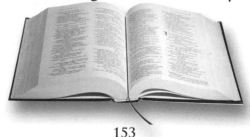

One of the most inspiring moments in Olympic history was Derek Redmond's semifinal run in the 1992
Barcelona Olympic Games.[1] Ever since his childhood,
Derek had dreamed of running in the Olympic Games.
Derek's time trials were extraordinary, and many
believed he was bound to win the individual gold in
the 400-meter race.

The moment arrived. Derek took his position. The
shot was fired, and the runners were off! Derek's first 200
meters were remarkable. At this pace he could sense that
his life's dream would come true. Suddenly a sharp pain
coursed through his leg. He slowed down and fell forward
onto the track. He had torn a hamstring, one of the most
painful injuries known in the world of sports.

With every tenth of a second Derek's dream was dying.
Medical personnel ran toward him in an effort to assist
him. Defiantly, Derek sprang to his feet as a sharp pain
shot through his entire leg. He began hopping forward
even though the pain was unbearable. All he would have
to do was fall down, and the medical staff would carry
him off.

Derek was determined to make the finish line, however!
As he approached the final stretch he felt a hand touch
him from behind. A voice said, "You don't have to do this."
Instantly Derek recognized that this was the voice of his
father, who had leaped from the grandstands.

Clasping his teeth in pain, he replied to his father, "Yes,
I do!"

His father responded, "Well then, we're going to finish this together." As they embraced tightly, Derek began crying uncontrollably.

As father and son struggled along the track together, many of the 70,000 in the grandstands realized the gravity of the moment—a runner had lost his dream. However, those in the grandstands realized something more important—the love of a father and son. Somehow the reality of this latter relationship made everything all right. When Derek and his father finally crossed the finish line, all 70,000 present rose and gave a standing ovation. Derek recalled the occasion of his injury with these touching words, "I hated the world. Then I felt a hand on my shoulder."

In Philippians 3 Paul invoked the imagery of running a race in order to encourage believers to strive towards life's finish line. The story of Derek Redmond, along with his life's goal and painful experiences, illustrates well the struggles of the believers in Philippi as they pressed on toward the finish line of life. Paul described in his Letter to the Philippians how he likewise had not yet reached his goal but nevertheless did not give up. He pressed on despite the struggles he encountered—in his current imprisonment and in light of the opponents to the truth of the gospel. Paul continued in his earthly struggles and encouraged the Philippian believers to do the same. With every step closer toward the finish line, Paul desired to know Christ more fully, for that, he indicated, was his greatest reward.

PHILIPPIANS 3:1–14

1Finally, my brethren, rejoice in the Lord. To write the same things again is no trouble to me, and it is a safeguard for you.

2Beware of the dogs, beware of the evil workers, beware of the false circumcision; **3**for we are the true circumcision, who worship in the Spirit of God and glory in Christ Jesus and put no confidence in the flesh, **4**although I myself might have confidence even in the flesh. If anyone else has a mind to put confidence in the flesh, I far more: **5**circumcised the eighth day, of the nation of Israel, of the tribe of Benjamin, a Hebrew of Hebrews; as to the Law, a Pharisee; **6**as to zeal, a persecutor of the church; as to the righteousness which is in the Law, found blameless.

7But whatever things were gain to me, those things I have counted as loss for the sake of Christ. **8**More than that, I count all things to be loss in view of the surpassing value of knowing Christ Jesus my Lord, for whom I have suffered the loss of all things, and count them but rubbish so that I may gain Christ, **9**and may be found in Him, not having a righteousness of my own derived from the Law, but that which is through faith in Christ, the righteousness which comes from God on the basis of faith, **10**that I may know Him and the power of His resurrection and the fellowship of His sufferings, being conformed to His death; **11**in order that I may attain to the resurrection from the dead.

12Not that I have already obtained it or have already become perfect, but I press on so that I may lay hold of that for which also I was laid hold of by Christ Jesus. **13**Brethren, I do not regard myself as having laid hold of it yet; but one thing I do: forgetting what lies behind and reaching forward to what lies ahead, **14**I press on toward the goal for the prize of the upward call of God in Christ Jesus.

Values in Light of the World (3:1–6)

Chapter 3 represents a slight transition from Paul's previous discussion concerning church unity and Christlike humility in chapters 1 and 2. Such digressions were common in ancient writings.[2] Many English translations start verse 1 with the word "finally" (see NASB, NRSV, NIV, KJV). This might lead one to believe that Paul was about to conclude his letter. However, the Greek word often translated as "finally," *loipon*, here in verse 1 is better translated as *well then* or *so*. In addition, *loipon* again appears in Philippians 4:8, thereby showing once more that Paul was not yet wrapping up his thoughts in chapter 3.

Paul introduced the transition in chapter 3 with the admonition to "rejoice in the Lord." This admonition refers back to Philippians 2:17–18. There Paul wrote that to suffer on behalf of the gospel and the Philippians was his joy, and he invited the believers in Philippi to rejoice with him in his circumstances. Likewise, the

Philippian believers now ought to hold on to joy amidst their situation.

Paul next swiftly turned to warning the Philippians concerning false teachers who might enter their midst without warning. In his following statements (3:2) one can note that Paul was charged with emotion as he described these teachers.

In verse 2, Paul three times used the word "beware." He labeled the false teachers "dogs," "evil workers," and "of the false circumcision." Dogs were considered unclean animals and signified those outside God's covenant.[3] Paul critiqued the self-righteous works of the opponents by calling their works "evil," a designation for works originating from the powers of darkness.

A third label that Paul employed for the false teachers is those belonging to "the false circumcision." By way of a wordplay, he used the Greek word *katatome*, meaning *to cut off* or *to mutilate*, to refer to circumcision in verse 2. The regular Greek word for circumcision is *peritome*, meaning *to cut around*. One can imagine the insult this wordplay posed. Paul noted that true circumcision in the new covenant is of the heart. Any other type of religious or social circumcision was in Paul's eyes a form of mutilation since it missed God's ultimate purpose of saving and changing persons into new creations in Christ.

Since Paul began the warning with the word "beware," it is likely that these Jewish-Christian opponents were not presently in the church. Rather, they might have been traveling teachers who entered churches and taught Old Testament customs such as being circumcised so as to assure one of maintaining eternal life (note in 3:10–11 that Paul taught a wholly different prerequisite for eternal life, namely *knowing Christ*).

In verses 3 and 4, Paul, in keeping with the subject matter, described the true circumcision—those who know Jesus Christ and worship in the Spirit of God. He next condemned the false teachers' tendencies toward placing "confidence . . . in the flesh." If anyone could claim heritage that warranted "confidence . . . in the flesh," he, Paul, had a greater claim.

Paul's credentials "in the flesh" indeed were impressive. In verse 5, he established his credentials as the most legitimate of Jews, "a Hebrew of Hebrews." That expression typically refers to one who was born in Palestine. He was also "a Pharisee." Next, he established his credentials as the most zealous of Jews (3:6). Thus Paul insisted that he was a greater authority on Judaism than these traveling Jewish-Christian teachers.

Values in Light of the Cross (3:7–11)

In verse 7, Paul drew a stark comparison between what counts in the eyes of the world, even the religious world (3:5–6), and what counts with regard to knowing Christ in the most intimate way possible. He considered all as loss compared to knowing Christ Jesus. The values in which Paul once placed his confidence were not necessarily evil. However, the value of knowing Christ had diminished, even nullified, all other values in his life.

The Greek verb translated "I have counted" in verse 7 is in the perfect tense. Therefore, it carries the idea that the action was completed in the past with the consequences of that action ongoing in the present. Thus, at some particular point in time in the past Paul had counted the "things," that is, the worldly values, as loss compared to knowing Christ. This value of knowing Christ had a continuous impact on him in his walk with the Lord. Through Paul's conversion on the Damascus road, he had made a conscious decision to exchange his worldly values for the values of the cross (Acts 9:8).

Philippians 3:8–11 provides additional force to the point concerning his losses that Paul made in verse 7. Starting with the words "More than that," or *yes indeed,* Paul in reality said, *I will tell you even more strongly why I rearranged my values in this manner.* Not only did he count his Jewish heritage and personal accomplishments as loss, but he counted "all things" as loss.

Some scholars have suggested that the kind of "knowing" (Greek, *gnosis*) that Paul mentioned in verse 8 might hint at a Hellenistic (Greek) form of religion.[4] However, Paul's understanding of *gnosis* or knowledge most likely refers to an Old Testament understanding of knowledge as a relationship with God (see Exodus 33:13). Not only did

Paul count the previous things as "loss," but he considered them "loss" on a daily basis. Ultimately, he counted all things as "rubbish" (more specifically, *excrement*) compared to the exceeding value of having a relationship with Jesus Christ.

In Philippians 3:9, Paul testified to his most passionate life pursuit, that he "may be found in Him, not having a righteousness of my own derived from the Law, but that which is though faith in Jesus Christ. . . . " Thus, according to Paul, only righteousness derived from God is valid.

One might wonder why Paul used a seemingly ambiguous expression in verse 10 when he wrote "that I may know Him." Had Paul not come to know the risen Lord even since his conversion on the Damascus road? Indeed, he had started a relationship with Christ by grace through faith and had sought ever since to know Christ more intimately. Paul's reference to knowing Christ and "the power of His resurrection and the fellowship of His sufferings" (3:10) represents Paul's maturing from personal conversion to becoming a suffering minister. The statement also expresses the need for resurrection power in daily Christian living.

The "fellowship of His sufferings" was a common concept to the people of God during Old Testament times. Of old, the Jewish people had associated suffering with the coming of Messiah (Acts 14:22). This seeking of fellowship with suffering did not mean that Paul sought martyrdom. Rather, Paul would have considered suffering an honor and an opportunity for deeper intimacy with Christ. Paul expressed this longing for deeper intimacy by using the expression "being conformed." Paul stated that he longed to be conformed to Christ's death rather than to his own previous worldly values. Note that the verb form is passive, "being comformed." Thus the action is being done to the subject, Paul, by an outside agent—the Holy Spirit. The action is of the ongoing kind, a conformation that is continuous in nature. Paul declared that he was continually being conformed by the Holy Spirit to the daily value of knowing Christ fully.

In verse 11 Paul provided a reason for his statements in verse 10. The apostle looked futuristically toward the Second Coming of Christ when the bodily resurrection will occur. In various English translations verse 11 may appear to make Paul doubtful about his participation in this future bodily resurrection at the Second Coming of Christ. Does this meant that Paul's eternal security depended on his actions? Note that verse 11 states, "that I may attain. . . ." The Greek word behind these words is *eipos*, which is an expression of expectation. To which expectation was Paul referring? Was he referring to afterlife or to the manner in which he might enter afterlife? Within the Letter of Philippians alone, even apart from looking at Greek grammar, to consider 3:11 as conveying doubt would contradict 1:23 and 3:9. Paul appears to have been certain of his participation in the future resurrection but perhaps expressed uncertainty concerning the manner by which he would reach that point—through martyrdom, through another form of death, or through being alive at the coming of Christ (see 1:20–26).[5]

Values in Light of the Highest Goal (3:12–14)

In verse 11 Paul had noted his life's goal as being to know Christ fully. In verse 12 he clarified that he had not yet reached that point of full understanding, or perfection, by any means. Perhaps his opponents, the false teachers in Philippi, claimed to have reached perfection. Paul indirectly objected to the pride of these opponents. Only a personal relationship with Christ moves one toward this perfection. Paul humbly recognized that he was dependent on his Lord and merely claimed his intention to lay hold of knowing Christ fully.

In verses 13–14 Paul used the analogy of ancient athletic games to illustrate his determination to seek authentic pure and mature faith. In these games the runners would line up in straight rows, run forward to a point in the arena, and then run back to a designated finish line.[6] Likewise, Paul's race to "know Christ" fully and thus be fully mature was a forward-looking race. He was determined not to look backward during his race. In actual racing the runner might lose valuable time looking backward. Once a race was completed, the winner would be called up and receive the prize (note the similar wording in verse 14).[7] This prize in the Christian life is to know Christ fully.

Implications and Actions

In Philippians 3:1–14 Paul shared from his personal life
a much needed perspective—life must be lived in light of
the highest goal of knowing Christ fully. No earthly value,
whether heritage, achievements, or even moral virtue,
will ever match up to the far exceeding value of knowing
Christ Jesus intimately.

Paul's decision to count former values as loss had been
a conscious decision with daily impact on his life. Paul
had never looked back in regret. Instead, he looked forward with courage and in a spirit of joy. He invited the
Philippians to do so likewise.

We too are encouraged to live our lives in a forward-
looking manner, focused on knowing Christ fully. Are we
able to say with Paul that we count all other things loss?
Do we count them loss with a spirit of joy, knowing that
with each step forward we are closer to the finish line,
closer to knowing Christ more fully if we truly surrender
our lives to him?

CIRCUMCISION

In the Old Testament, circumcision was initiated with the
covenant with Abraham (Genesis 17:10–14). Males were to
be circumcised on the eighth day as a sign of that covenant.
For proselytes (Gentiles who desired to follow the Jewish

religion) circumcision was one of the main conditions for entry into the Jewish community.

In time, circumcision not only became known as a religious rite but also became the mark of a truly Jewish man. Since the time of the Maccabean Revolt (occurring between the Old and New Testaments, a time of great threat to the Jews) circumcision took on the social function of an identity marker.

In the early church, some Jewish Christians insisted that Gentile males had to be circumcised. This circumcision then was not merely a religious matter but rather an issue of believers identifying with the Jewish community. Paul held to the position that those who are of the true circumcision—that is, those who have their identity and loyalty focused on the cross of Christ—are the ones who truly belong to God.

RIGHTEOUSNESS AND FAITH:

Righteousness and faith are connected. In Philippians 3:9, Paul's true righteousness comes from God and is dependent on faith.[8] Our right standing before God likewise comes from our relationship with Christ. His faithfulness unto the cross enabled our faith in him and leads us back to God.

QUESTIONS

1. In Philippians 3:8 Paul stated that he counted everything "loss." This perspective appears to go beyond his Jewish heritage and personal achievements. He implied that he gave up more than that. What do you think Paul could have meant? How does Paul's perspective relate to our perspective?

2. What are practical ways in which believers can seek to know Christ fully day by day?

3. How can morally neutral values in life (such as hobbies or clubs) become values that become our confidence and security, putting Christ in a secondary role?

4. How can we avoid placing our trust in worldly values and instead focus on values of the cross?

N O T E S

1. See
   http://sports.espn.go.com/espn/espn25/story?page=moments/94
   and also www.derekredmond.com.

2. Craig S. Keener, *The IVP Bible Background Commentary: New Testament* (Downers Grove, Illinois: InterVarsity Press, 1993), 562.

3. Keener, 562.

4. Peter T. O'Brien. *The Epistle to the Philippians*, The New International Greek Commentary (Grand Rapids, Michigan: William B. Eerdmans Publishing Company, 1991), 387–388.

5. O'Brien, 413.

6. Keener, 564.

7. Kenner, 564.

8 "Righteousness, Righteousness of God," *Dictionary of Paul and His Letters* (Downers Grove, Illinois: InterVarsity Press, 1993).

LESSON ELEVEN

Rejoice in the Lord

MAIN IDEA

We can learn and practice authentic ways for increasing our joy in life.

QUESTION TO EXPLORE

How can we live with greater joy?

STUDY AIM

To describe ways for truly rejoicing in the Lord

QUICK READ

Paul was imprisoned but found joy in thinking of the believers in Philippi. By not focusing on his circumstances, Paul viewed life through the lens of contentment and joy.

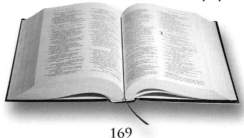

All of his life David Livingstone (1813–1873) longed to
serve God. Born in Scotland, he took his family to Africa
for mission work. Within a few days one of his children
died. He took his family back to Scotland and returned
to Africa alone. His wife and children did not see him for
five long years. While he was in Africa, he was mauled by
a lion. Too, he was blinded in one eye because of an acci-
dent. Returning on furlough, he still decided to return to
Africa, and his family agreed.

A few more years went by, and David invited his wife
to join him in Africa. The same day she set foot on the
African continent, she contracted a crippling African disease. He ended up burying his wife in Africa.

Livingstone was asked whether he thought his sacrifice was worth the outcome. He answered:

> For my own part, I have never ceased to rejoice
> that God has appointed me to such an office.
> People talk of the sacrifice I have made in spend-
> ing so much of my life in Africa. Can that be called
> a sacrifice which is simply paid back as a small
> part of a great debt owing to our God, which we
> can never repay? Is that a sacrifice which brings
> its own blest reward in healthful activity, the con-
> sciousness of doing good, peace of mind, and a
> bright hope of a glorious destiny hereafter? . . .
> It is emphatically no sacrifice. Say rather it is a
> privilege. Anxiety, sickness, suffering, or danger,

now and then, with a foregoing of the common conveniences and charities of this life, may make us pause, and cause the spirit to waver, and the soul to sink; but let this only be for a moment. All these are nothing when compared with the glory which shall be revealed in and for us. I never made a sacrifice.[1]

Paul likewise never ceased to rejoice that God had appointed him to the office of apostle to the Gentiles. Throughout his Letter to the Philippians, Paul encouraged the believers to rejoice despite their circumstances. As Paul was coming to the end of his letter, he continued to spur on the believers to rejoice.

Paul began his closing comments in chapter 4 of his Letter to the Philippians on a positive note, exhorting the Philippian believers to "stand firm in the Lord." This positive mood is interrupted, however, with concern for two women who could not reconcile their differences. Their discord illustrated for Paul the lack of unity and joy among the believers. In verse 3 he turned his attention for a brief moment to ask his "true companion" to help these two women reconcile. The identity of this "true companion" is unclear. Even so, the seriousness of the matter of discord within the church was obvious to Paul.

Paul deeply loved the Philippian church. The Philippians likewise deeply loved Paul and had sent Epaphroditus (Philippians 4:18) to minister to him. Paul rejoiced in the Philippians' concern for him even as he urged them to pursue unity.

PHILIPPIANS 4:4–20

4 Rejoice in the Lord always; again I will say, rejoice! **5**Let your gentle spirit be known to all men. The Lord is near. **6**Be anxious for nothing, but in everything by prayer and supplication with thanksgiving let your requests be made known to God. **7**And the peace of God, which surpasses all comprehension, will guard your hearts and your minds in Christ Jesus.

8Finally, brethren, whatever is true, whatever is honorable, whatever is right, whatever is pure, whatever is lovely, whatever is of good repute, if there is any excellence and if anything worthy of praise, dwell on these things. **9**The things you have learned and received and heard and seen in me, practice these things, and the God of peace will be with you.

10But I rejoiced in the Lord greatly, that now at last you have revived your concern for me; indeed, you were concerned before, but you lacked opportunity. **11**Not that I speak from want, for I have learned to be content in whatever circumstances I am. **12**I know how to get along with humble means, and I also know how to live in prosperity; in any and every circumstance I have learned the secret of being filled and going hungry, both of having abundance and suffering need. **13**I can do all things through Him who strengthens me. **14**Nevertheless, you have done well to share with me in my affliction.

15You yourselves also know, Philippians, that at the first preaching of the gospel, after I left Macedonia, no church shared with me in the matter of giving and receiving but you alone; **16**for even in Thessalonica you sent a gift more than once for my needs. **17**Not that I seek the gift itself, but I seek for the profit which increases to your account. **18**But I have received everything in full and have an abundance; I am amply supplied, having received from Epaphroditus what you have sent, a fragrant aroma, an acceptable sacrifice, well-pleasing to God. **19**And my God will supply all your needs according to His riches in glory in Christ Jesus. **20**Now to our God and Father [be] the glory forever and ever. Amen.

True Joy Is Public (4:4–7)

Paul turned his address again to the believers as a group by using plural parts of speech in Greek. He urged the Philippian Christians to rejoice in the Lord on all occasions. Paul continued in the instructive mode, coaching the Christians to let their "gentle spirit" be known to all people (Phil. 4:5). Gentleness is a characteristic of the church that should be public. The phrase, "The Lord is near" (4:5), intensifies the encouragement to regain unity.

At first glance, verse 6 may appear to be an abrupt shift of thought from the previous exhortation toward unity and evangelism. However, "Be anxious for nothing" (4:6), or more accurately, *Stop being anxious for nothing*, fits the circumstances of the Philippian believers and Paul himself. The believers faced internal challenges of church disunity and external challenges by false teachers, and Paul was in prison. The word Paul used to denote anxiety in verse 6 conveys the sense of having unreasonable concerns, worrying about items outside the realm of control. Paul had discussed in this letter thus far how to approach problems of unity with humility (chapter 2) and how to know Christ more fully (chapter 3). Now he called the Philippian Christians to rejoice in the Lord regardless of circumstances. Those who know the Lord always have reason to rejoice in their salvation and let that joy be public.

The alternative, or solution, to unnecessary anxiety consists of three modes of prayer along with thanksgiving, "In everything by prayer and supplication, with thanksgiving let your requests be made know to God. . ." (4:6). Paul here used three different Greek words for prayer. The first Greek word, *proseuche*, translated "prayer," is used for prayer in general. Throughout the New Testament, however, the word regularly is used in the sense of petition for others, or intercession.[2] The second Greek word for prayer in verse 6, *deesis*, translated "supplication," refers to a humble pleading with

God for God's help. The third Greek word for prayer that Paul employs in verse 6, *aitema*, translated "requests," is used for specific requests.

The three modes of prayer must be voiced "with thanksgiving." Paul's solution for unnecessary anxiety is also to show gratitude in prayer. God will answer prayers in God's time. In the meantime, gratitude is to be the Christian's standard of behavior. We can always remember with joy and gratitude God's great gift of salvation in Jesus Christ.

According to Paul, if believers pray in the manner set forth in verse 6, the peace of God results (3:7). An enlightening description of God's peace follows. God's peace "surpasses all comprehension." The word translated "surpasses" is derived from the word for *excellent*. The phrase thus can be rendered peace that *excels beyond all knowledge*. God's peace, which results from refusing to worry and from praying fervently, excels above all attempts people typically make in trying to find peace. God's supernatural peace will "guard" the hearts and minds of the Philippians. The term translated "guard," *phroureo*, is part of military terminology and denotes an army guarding a city. The city of Philippi was guarded by a military garrison at the time and thus the metaphor would have been understood easily. Peace is not viewed as a passive feeling but an active work of protective heavenly powers on behalf of God's children.

True Joy Is Focused (4:8–9)

The series of admonitions with which Paul began in 4:1 is wrapped up in verses 8 and 10 with a focus on moral virtues. For Paul the outcome of having joy in the Lord is a joy that is focused. He listed six ethical qualities that are of such magnitude that the Apostle insisted that the believers ought to let their minds "dwell on" these qualities (4:8). The Greek verb tense of the word translated "dwell on" indicates letting their minds "dwell on" these qualities continually. The overall condition to these virtues is two-fold—"if there is any excellence and if anything worthy of praise" (4:8). According to Greek grammar, the "if" should be understood as *since.* Thus the expression could be translated as, *since there is excellence and things worthy of praise in these virtues,* "dwell on these things."

The qualities in verse 8 ("whatever is true, whatever is honorable, whatever is right, whatever is pure, whatever is lovely, whatever is of good repute") were not unique to Christianity. Rather, these qualities were part of the culture of that day.[3] The philosophers would teach these Greek virtues and encourage the people to focus on them. Paul would have known that the Philippians were familiar with these virtues and deemed them important as well. However, he wrote that these virtues were valid only in the context of what the believers had "learned and received and heard and seen in me" (4:9). That which the believers in Philippi had learned, received, heard, and seen in Paul was the gospel. Focusing on moral virtues is meaningful only when done so in the context of the good news of Jesus Christ.

True Joy Is Content (4:10–13)

Paul next wrote that he rejoiced greatly about the concern the Philippians had shown to him (4:10). The focus of Paul's rejoicing, or the sphere of his rejoicing, was "in the Lord."

In verse 11 Paul wrote of his contentment. He could rejoice in the Lord because he was content. The Stoics taught that people should be self-sufficient. Paul spoke of reliance on God. Thus, Paul's contentment was based on relying on God. He continued by describing how he had learned contentment in every situation as related to his current circumstances.

Paul shared how he learned this contentment in verse 12. He wrote that he knew how to "get along with humble means, and . . . how to live in prosperity" (4:13). The phrase translated "I know" comes from the Greek word *oida*.[4] *Oida* in verse 12 signifies the manner in which Paul knew to live. Thus Paul was "explaining that he knows *how* to live in an appropriate manner under these circumstances: he knows how to be brought low by poverty or want and to be content."[5] This knowledge was not gained easily. Paul stated that he had "learned the secret" to being content. The Greek word for "learned" indicates that the learning took place at some time in the past. Paul also added that this learning took place "in any and every circumstance" (4:12). Paul learned the secret of contentment amidst his circumstances, "being filled and going hungry, both of having abundance and suffering need" (4:12).

The power of Christ enabled Paul to learn this contentment in his circumstances. He therefore declared that he could "do all things through Him who strengthens" him (4:13). This "all" is tempered by the context. Paul spoke of his specific circumstances in specific contexts. Furthermore, the "all" refers to Paul's ability to be content in the specific circumstances in the specific contexts—times of abundance (when Paul had means to provide for needs in the ministry) and times of need (such as when he was imprisoned).

True Joy Is Shared (4:14–20)

In verses 14–20 Paul thanked the Philippians for the gift they had sent with Epaphroditus. In ancient Mediterranean culture, reciprocity was a key social feature. Thus one can observe Paul noting the gift as the Philippians reciprocating his investment in their lives. Paul expressed his gratefulness for the Philippians sharing in his affliction (4:14). The reference to his affliction likely refers to his imprisonment, which was related to his ministry to the church in Philippi.[6]

In verses 15–16 Paul rejoiced in how the Philippian believers at previous times in his ministry had provided for him. In verse 17 Paul declared that he did not seek the gift but rather God's reciprocity toward the believers. Paul desired that the Philippians would share in the joy of God's spiritual blessings.

In verse 18 Paul turned to the use of sacrificial terminology—"a fragrant aroma, an acceptable sacrifice, well-pleasing to God." Paul assured the Philippians that he had been supplied in abundance with everything he needed. In response to the believers' love and friendship for Paul, Paul shared in a prayer-like fashion that God likewise could meet their needs in their circumstances (4:19). Whereas Paul now had abundance, God had far exceeding riches. Paul let his prayer flow over into a doxology in 4:20.

Implications and Actions

True joy is found first of all in believers' salvation. However, everyday joy stems from contentment despite one's circumstances. This contentment can be learned and once learned can be shared. Authentic joy is contagious and represents the gospel. Are you ready to learn and embrace true contentment leading to authentic daily joy in Christ?

CONTENTMENT

Greek philosophers near Paul's time taught that people should be self-sufficient, able to take care of themselves. Thus like the virtues listed in Philippians 4:8, contentment (Phil. 4:11) was a virtue as well. One ancient Greek teacher of philosophy, Epictetus, wrote, "A man should also be prepared to be sufficient unto himself—to dwell with himself alone, even as God dwells with Himself alone. . . ."[7]

Contentment, or self-sufficiency, is "independent of external circumstances . . . ."[8] Paul redefined this well-known virtue as *independence from external circumstances through reliance on God*. He explained that Christ provided him the strength to learn contentment amidst his circumstances (4:13). Thus, contentment can be learned. One can learn to rely on God in the strength of Christ and be content despite external circumstances.

PAX ROMANA AND PEACE OF GOD

The "peace of God" (Phil. 4:7) forms a sharp contrast to the Roman concept of *Pax Romana*, the peace of Rome. The Roman empire used *Pax Romana* as a philosophy of tolerance, better defined as *the absence of trouble*. Paul used the Greek word *eirene* when speaking of peace. This peace of God far exceeds external circumstances. Too, *eirene* conveys a sense of tranquility.[9] Paul's use of *eirene* overlaps with the concept of *shalom* in the Old Testament. *Shalom* conveys the idea of wholeness.

Thus, God's peace brings internal wholeness and tranquility, whereas the peace of the world is external and temporal at best. Ultimately, the peace of God transcends this life for those who know Christ.

QUESTIONS

1. Why is prayer often a last resort for many people? How can we change our attitude in practical ways about this?

2. How can the thought of Philippians 4:13 be misused? How should we interpret and apply the verse?

3. In what areas of life is being content a challenge for you?

4. Should we ever be discontented? Is there such a concept as *holy discontent*?

5. When have you met a person whom you expected
   to be most miserable given his or her circumstances
   and yet the person turned out to be content and have
   true joy—not fake or superficial happiness, but real
   joy?

NOTES

1. Statement by David Livingstone, Cambridge University, December 4, 1857.

2. Peter T. O'Brien, *The New International Greek Commentary: The Epistle to the Philippians* (Grand Rapids, Michigan: William B. Eerdmans Publishing Company, 1991), 492.

3. Gerald F. Hawthorne, *Philippians*, Word Biblical Commentary (Waco, Texas: Word Books Publisher, 1983), 188.

4. See lesson 8 on 1:19–21.

5. O'Brien, 523, italics in original.

6. O'Brien, 529.

7. Epictetus, *The Golden Sayings of Epictetus,* XCVIII.

8. Hawthorne, 198.

9 "Eirene," 22.42. *Greek-English Lexicon of the New Testament Based on Semantic Domains.* Eds. Johannes P. Louw and Eugene A. Nida. Vols. 1 & 2 (New York: United Bible Societies, 1989).

───── U N I T   T H R E E ─────

The Letter to the Colossians

As we continue this study of "Living with Faithfulness and Joy," we find further resources in the Letter to the Colossians. We will see in the Book of Colossians that Paul addressed the power and authority of Christ and called for faithfulness in our relationship to him.

Our world is filled with many people who affirm that Jesus was a good teacher, a great man, and even a revolutionary leader. Some people insist that Christ is but one of many religious options.

The Colossian Christians also lived in a world with many religious options. The Christians to whom Paul addressed this letter lived in a world in which the gods were fickle and could be out-smarted by human effort. Paul wanted the Colossians to understand that Christ could not be overcome by human whims, but that Christ was the all-powerful Creator of the universe.

Various suggestions have been made about why the Colossian Christians needed to be reminded of the important truth that Christ is supreme. Perhaps the church was being challenged by religious and philosophical ideas that swirled about in the first-century world and that would have been found in the Greco-Roman culture of Colosse (Colossians 2:8).[1] Perhaps the challenge came from the Jews there. They may have insisted that keeping the Jewish laws and rituals was important and thus had drawn some Christians into, or back into, such practices (Col. 2:16–23). Perhaps what was misleading the Colossian Christians was a mixture of these influences. We do not know for sure.

Colosse was located in the Roman province of Asia, in the western portion of modern Turkey. The city was located about 100 miles east of Ephesus, a journey of several days in the first century. Paul may never have visited Colosse in person (2:1), but his influence apparently reached there prior to this letter. When Paul preached in Ephesus for two years, "all the Jews and Greeks who lived in the province of Asia heard the word of the Lord" (Acts 19:10). "All the Jews and Greeks who lived in the province of Asia" would have included the people of Colosse. Paul also had close contact with the neighboring town of Laodicea, only ten miles away (Col. 2:1; 4:13, 15–16). So Paul knew the Colossians well and cared deeply for them (1:3–4; 2:1).

Several verses in this letter suggest Paul was in prison when he wrote it (4:3, 10, 18). The traditional view is that Paul wrote Colossians toward the end of his ministry, around the early 60s during his imprisonment in Rome (Acts 28:30–31).

The lessons in this unit are from Colossians 1—2. In lessons six and seven of our study of Ephesians, we studied passages that were quite similar to the emphases in Colossians 3—4. For this reason, we will not repeat those emphases.

UNIT THREE. COLOSSIANS

N O T E S

1. Unless otherwise indicated, all Scripture quotations in this introduction and the lessons on Colossians are from the New International Version.

LESSON TWELVE

Recognize Christ's Supremacy

MAIN IDEA

Christ is the supreme revelation of God, Lord over creation and the church, and the One by whom God provides reconciliation.

QUESTION TO EXPLORE

How can we say Christ is supreme in a world of many religions?

STUDY AIM

To acknowledge Christ's supremacy and describe what it means for my life

QUICK READ

Paul makes clear that Christ is supreme over creation, the church, and individual believers. Paul also asserts that those who follow the supreme Christ are reconciled to God through Christ.

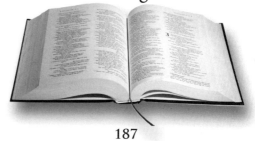

While my sons and I were on a recent trip to a local beach-side park, the two boys decided to play a game they called *stop the waves*. The game went like this. They would erect a sand wall only to have the waves knock it down. My oldest son would scream over the sound of pounding surf, "dig harder," as he passed the blame as usual to his younger brother. My youngest son was undaunted and continued to heap up sand with renewed vigor. On and on the game went, but not once did the waves stop rolling or the wall stop falling. Never did my little guys stop to ask themselves a very important question. *Could it be possible that we cannot stop the waves? Maybe the waves are just too powerful.* They saw themselves as masters of the surf. What they did not realize was that they were no match for the sheer force of the waves.

Could it be that when it comes to turning our lives over to Christ that we too erect walls of sand against the beating surf? But our walls are more effective than those built by my sons. Although Christ's power is supreme, he will not wash away our defenses. He loves us but will not intrude into our lives without our inviting him to do so. What keeps us from experiencing Christ's power is our will. We need to let Christ tear down the walls that we have built and let him have control of all we do. We need to let him be supreme in our lives.

Paul wrote to the Colossians to remind them of the true power and supremacy of Christ. Paul wanted them to realize the full extent of Christ's control. Many scholars believe that this section of Paul's letter is actually a hymn that was commonly sung in the early church. While they disagree as to specifics, like the number of stanzas and exactly what parts are the original hymn and which parts are Paul's explanation of it, most are certain that Paul intentionally inserted a hymn at this point. Why would Paul burst into song at the beginning of a letter?

One way of looking at what Paul did is by thinking about what was once a common occurrence in many churches. It was not uncommon for a music minister to stop a congregation in the middle of singing a hymn and to repeat slowly the words the congregation had just sung. *Do you hear the words?* the minister of music would say. *Do you really believe what you are singing?* Often, this was a way of trying to get us to sing louder, but the effect was to make us think about the meaning behind the words, what we really meant when we sang them.

Perhaps Paul had a similar idea in mind, saying to the Colossians in effect, *Do you hear the words? Do you really believe what you are singing?* By pointing the Colossians to a song they may have sung many times in worship, he was helping bring into focus the reality behind the words. Paul encourages us, too, to see the Christ who is Lord of creation, of the church, and of individual Christians.

COLOSSIANS 1:15–23

¹⁵He is the image of the invisible God, the firstborn over all creation. ¹⁶For by him all things were created: things in heaven and on earth, visible and invisible, whether thrones or powers or rulers or authorities; all things were created by him and for him. ¹⁷He is before all things, and in him all things hold together. ¹⁸And he is the head of the body, the church; he is the beginning and the firstborn from among the dead, so that in everything he might have the supremacy. ¹⁹For God was pleased to have all his fullness dwell in him, ²⁰and through him to reconcile to himself all things, whether things on earth or things in heaven, by making peace through his blood, shed on the cross.

²¹Once you were alienated from God and were enemies in your minds because of your evil behavior. ²²But now he has reconciled you by Christ's physical body through death to present you holy in his sight, without blemish and free from accusation—²³if you continue in your faith, established and firm, not moved from the hope held out in the gospel. This is the gospel that you heard and that has been proclaimed to every creature under heaven, and of which I, Paul, have become a servant.

Christ, the Lord of Creation (1:15–17)

Paul began his discussion of the supremacy of Christ in creation by declaring that Jesus is "the image of the invisible God" (Colossians 1:15). The English use of the word "image" may be unfortunate. Many of us hear "image" and imagine that Paul might have meant that Jesus was a reflection or representation of God. In much the same way, we might speak of seeing our image in a mirror. The problem with this type of thinking is that Paul did not intend to say that Christ is a reflection of God, but that Christ is the visible expression of the invisible God. Jesus is God in visible form. Through Christ, we see God. Christ's deity is not merely contained in his human form. He possesses all the power and authority of God because he is God. The point that Paul wished to make was that if Christ is God (and he is), and God created, then Christ also created.

Paul not only asserted that Christ is the visible expression of an invisible God, but he also claimed that Christ is "the firstborn over all creation" (Col. 1:15). If Paul were speaking of Jesus' actual birth in Bethlehem, then we must wonder at the expression "firstborn." Likewise, because Christ is God and God is eternal and without beginning, it would be incorrect to speak of Christ as being born at all. What Paul intended here is that Christ is the "firstborn" in relation to his inheritance. He has all the rights of the firstborn son. What Paul proclaimed was that in the same way that a firstborn son in an Israelite family would inherit the position of his father, Christ also inherited everything from the Father. All that is the Father's is Christ's. Thus Christ exercises the power and authority of the Father.

Paul wanted us to affirm with him that Christ is God and that he has all the powers attributable to God. Paul made this clearer when he stated: by "him [Jesus] all things were created" (1:16). Paul intended for us to understand that Jesus was responsible for all of creation, and so he made it clear that Christ created the heavens and the earth, the visible and the invisible. By asserting that Jesus created all things, Paul was claiming that Jesus has power over all things, not just the material world but the supernatural world as well. The dominions, rulers, and authorities that he mentioned are part of this invisible world. Interestingly, in today's world, some Christians have become wrapped up in worries about the supernatural. In such an environment it becomes possible for us to become so focused on "demonic" or other powers that we forget that Christ has power over all these things. There is nothing visible or invisible that Christ cannot conquer. Could it be that our concerns about those things in the external world are really the result of not recognizing the power Christ has over all creation? This is the Christ through whom and for whom all things were created.

Christ is the God who created all things, who has the power and authority over all things, and if this were not enough, Paul stated that "in him [Christ] all things hold together" (1:17). The very fabric of the universe is held together through the power of Christ. When we wake up in the morning, it is through the power of Christ. When the sun rises, it is because of the power of Christ. When a child is born, it is through the power of Christ. In small ways and small things that go unnoticed, the power of Christ is exercised in our daily lives. The world works because Christ holds it together.

Christ, the Lord of the Church (1:18–19)

Some might say that Paul could have simply stopped with saying that Christ is God and that he created all things. But Paul wanted us to understand that Jesus is not some generic creator who created the world and then left it to its own devices. The Greek and Roman gods were very much these types of gods. Jesus, however, was the true God, and he expected not only to be seen as Creator but also to be seen as Head of the church. When Paul said that Jesus was Head of the church he was saying nothing less than that Jesus must be actively and daily in charge of the church. Christ is not an absentee ruler but is present and active, leading from his place at the head of the congregation. Paul asserted this by saying that Jesus is the "beginning, the firstborn from among the dead" (1:18). The church was formed when Christ defeated death and rose from the grave. In forming the church, Christ took his place at the head of the church.

Few Christians would argue against the premise that Christ is the Head of the church. But the question remains, do we really give Christ control? Are our worship services,

Bible study classes, and fellowships truly for Christ, or are they for us? In a day and age when a common reason offered for changing churches is *I just was not getting fed*, can we really say the focus is on Christ? When we make church decisions based on what is most comfortable for us rather than on what would most please Christ, are we truly affirming the leadership of Christ? When our church meetings are controlled by bickering and politics, are we truly listening to Christ? Paul insisted that Christ is not just Head of the church in theory but that he is Head of the church in reality.

Christ, the Lord of the Individual Christian (1:20–23)

Paul was not content with our knowing that Christ is Lord of creation and Lord of the church. He also wanted us to understand that Christ is Lord of each and every one of us who call ourselves believers. We are who we are because Christ and Christ alone died for our sins. The basic teaching of Scripture is that because we were incapable of ever being good enough to restore our broken relationship with God, Christ came and died for us. He came because of our inability to resist sin. God's just nature required punishment for sin, thus leaving no opening for a restored relationship with God. However, Christ, the Creator of the universe, the firstborn, and the image of God came and took that punishment upon himself. Because Christ died, we are able to be forgiven, restored, and reconciled to God. This act was not merely a generic act for people or for the church but was a personal act for you and for me as individuals.

What then does all this have to do with Jesus' supremacy? Christ could have claimed authority over us simply because he created us. He could have claimed authority over us because he holds the highest position within the church. But Christ's ultimate authority does not rest with these claims but with his act of unselfish love. Christ is Lord, ruler, and supreme leader of our lives because he was willing to give all for us. In effect we were bought and paid for by Jesus, not in a cheap, oppressive sense, but in a loving, giving way. Christ can claim supreme authority in our lives because Christ alone has given himself for us. He alone has died for something we did wrong. Jesus is Lord because all that we are in those dark places of our heart he took upon himself and all the innocence that he held within himself he has given to us. Christ's authority in our lives is based not on a dictatorial demand to recognize Christ's power but on an urgent plea to recognize Christ's love.

Jesus cannot be given second place in our lives. We cannot worship Christ and at the same time worship something else. Worship means offering our supreme allegiance. No one else has died to reconcile us to God. If Christ's death is the only way to be reconciled to God, then Christ alone must be the supreme center of our faith. We cannot mix our faith in Jesus with a belief in the equal claims of other religions. When it comes to being reconciled with God, there are no other paths apart from Christ.

Implications and Actions

Do you ever stop and ask where Christ is in the midst of your decisions? Where is Christ in the midst of your life?

Christ wants us to remember that he is the Lord of creation. Nothing can come against us if Christ determines to keep it from us. Christ wants us to remember that all things hold together in him, that our breath and our life rest in his power. Christ deserves recognition for the unacknowledged ways he is present in our daily lives. He wants us to remember that he is Head of the church because he alone made the church possible through his death.

When we worship, fellowship, and conduct business, we must place the emphasis on Christ and not our own desires and wishes. Christ wants us to remember that it is he, and he alone, who has restored us to God. Paul gave us a hymn on the supremacy of Christ and in effect asked, *Do you really believe the words you are singing?*

PERSEVERANCE OF THE SAINTS

Baptists have long held to what is called *the perseverance of the saints*. The meaning of this phrase is that once you were saved you could not lose your salvation. Paul's statement in Colossians 1:22–23 seems, at face value, to imply that *if* you are steadfast then you will be *presented holy* to God (1:22). If you do not remain steadfast, one might assume that you could lose your salvation. The key to understanding this verse rests in the tone of what Paul is saying. Paul did not seem to doubt that the Colossian Christians would stand fast in their faith. The verse serves as a reminder with the rest of the passage to put Christ first.

Paul could very well have been talking directly to a group of people who claimed the faith but who had not embraced Christ for who he truly was. These might have been individuals who claimed Christ as well as other gods or who did not believe in the divinity of Christ. These persons, although appearing to have faith, were in fact not Christians at all.

MAKING CHRIST SUPREME IN YOUR LIFE

- Look at the things in your life that frighten, confuse, or bother you. Give those things over in prayer to Christ, who has power over all things.

- Decide today to give your church and your role in it over to Christ. Ask what you can do in the church to place the focus on Jesus and take it off yourself.

- Give yourself over to the love Christ has offered you. Then, realizing that Christ wants only the best for you, give over every part of your life to him.

QUESTIONS

1. Since Christ truly has power over things both visible and invisible, what does that say about your personal fears, problems, or sense of oppression?

2. Can you name some ways in which Christ holds your life together? How ought you to respond to any unacknowledged ways that Christ is daily present in your life?

3. Reflecting on your involvement at church, in what ways is your involvement truly about Christ? In what ways does your involvement in church seem to be more about you?

4. How much of Christ's love do you recognize, and how does the love of Christ affect your ability to turn your life fully over to him? What areas of your life are you still holding onto?

FOCAL TEXT
Colossians 2:6–23

BACKGROUND
Colossians 2:6–23

LESSON THIRTEEN

Focus On the Real, Not Spiritual Gimmickry

MAIN IDEA

Focus on Christ and beware
of spiritual gimmickry.

QUESTION TO EXPLORE

What spiritual gimmicks do people
sometimes rely on when a genuine
relationship with Christ is what
they need and all they need?

STUDY AIM

To resolve to focus on the real,
Christ, rather than to rely on the
spiritual gimmickry of rules, rituals,
and cultural beliefs and practices

QUICK READ

Paul addressed strange ideas
among the Colossian believers
and encouraged them to hold to
their relationship with Christ,
not to the false practices they
had been tempted to embrace.

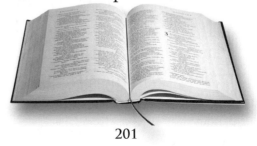

With new diseases seeming to crop up every year, doctors sometimes come across a sick patient with an illness they cannot diagnose. They search in vain to place a name on the set of symptoms their patient experiences. That does not, however, keep the doctors from treating the symptoms until they know the disease to which the symptoms point.

Reading Colossians 2:6–23 is a lot like being a doctor who can see the symptoms but cannot diagnose the disease. We have only the record of one side of a debate. Paul clearly knew there was a problem with the Colossian church. Christians in Colosse had been assaulted with bad teaching that was causing the church to stumble. Paul did not tell us what person or group was responsible for the teaching. We are left without knowing who the opponent was. Paul did not give the false teaching a name either. He simply described and refuted the various problems with his opponent's arguments.

Not knowing who the opponent was has not kept scholars from speculating about a possible candidate. One of the earliest ideas was that Paul addressed a group of people who were caught between the Jewish and Gentile Christian camps. Bad theology was being promulgated by both sides. Others believe that Paul was dealing with a group that borrowed ideas from various belief systems and combined them into one. They refer to this group as *pre-Gnostic* since it has some of the characteristics of Gnosticism, which came later. Yet another group of scholars sees Paul's opponents as belonging to one of the mystery religions that were prevalent during that time. These religions were mostly secretive societies that were imported from other cultures. More recently, many scholars have embraced the idea that what Paul battled was simply a very austere and mystical form of Judaism similar to that practiced by the Qumran community (the community that produced the Dead Sea Scrolls).

That we do not know whom Paul battled does not stop us from understanding the symptoms Paul described and applying them to our own time and situation. We have already noted in the previous lesson that Paul opened his letter with a hymn on the supremacy of Christ. Paul would elaborate on this theme in Colossians 2 as he refuted the false teaching that was threatening the Colossian church. In the course of his debate, he would make three very basic claims. First and foremost, Christ alone in us is sufficient for us. Secondly, rituals and practices are no substitute for the presence of Christ. Finally, other supernatural powers are no substitute for the presence of Christ. In each of these discussions, Paul addressed the false views that led him to make these central points.

COLOSSIANS 2:6–23

6So then, just as you received Christ Jesus as Lord, continue to live in him, **7**rooted and built up in him, strengthened in the faith as you were taught, and overflowing with thankfulness.

[8]See to it that no one takes you captive through hollow and deceptive philosophy, which depends on human tradition and the basic principles of this world rather than on Christ.

[9]For in Christ all the fullness of the Deity lives in bodily form, [10]and you have been given fullness in Christ, who is the head over every power and authority. [11]In him you were also circumcised, in the putting off of the sinful nature, not with a circumcision done by the hands of men but with the circumcision done by Christ, [12]having been buried with him in baptism and raised with him through your faith in the power of God, who raised him from the dead.

[13]When you were dead in your sins and in the uncircumcision of your sinful nature, God made you alive with Christ. He forgave us all our sins, [14]having canceled the written code, with its regulations, that was against us and that stood opposed to us; he took it away, nailing it to the cross. [15]And having disarmed the powers and authorities, he made a public spectacle of them, triumphing over them by the cross.

[16]Therefore do not let anyone judge you by what you eat or drink, or with regard to a religious festival, a New Moon celebration or a Sabbath day. [17]These are a shadow of the things that were to come; the reality, however, is found in Christ. [18]Do not let anyone who delights in false humility and the worship of angels disqualify you for the prize. Such a person goes into great detail about what he has seen, and

his unspiritual mind puffs him up with idle notions. [19]He has lost connection with the Head, from whom the whole body, supported and held together by its ligaments and sinews, grows as God causes it to grow.

[20]Since you died with Christ to the basic principles of this world, why, as though you still belonged to it, do you submit to its rules: [21]"Do not handle! Do not taste! Do not touch!"? [22]These are all destined to perish with use, because they are based on human commands and teachings. [23]Such regulations indeed have an appearance of wisdom, with their self-imposed worship, their false humility and their harsh treatment of the body, but they lack any value in restraining sensual indulgence.

Christ Alone in Us Is Sufficient for Us (2:6–15)

Have you noticed the recent popularity of religion and spirituality in our society? You can purchase crosses in all shapes and sizes. You can buy a guardian angel at your local convenience store. Television talk show hosts discuss their latest spiritual insight in prime time. There was a time when the greatest threat to Christianity was that people would believe in too little. Today the threat to Christianity may be that people believe in too much that has no validity.

Paul wasted no time in stating his answer to the problem. The word "therefore" at the beginning of verse 6 alerts us to the fact that he was going to tell us what needed to be done. An army commander would have said it this way, *Just give me the bottom line up front, soldier.* Paul wrote: "as you received Christ Jesus the Lord, continue to live in him" (Colossians 2:6). Paul could not have been more direct than that. The Christ they had received was sufficient for them. Walking in him was sufficient for their lives.

Paul was concerned that the Colossians would be taken captive by false teaching and give themselves over to it instead of to Christ (Col. 2:8). Paul identified this false teaching as an empty philosophy built on human reason and not on divine revelation. It was the product of "the basic principles of this world" (2:8). When Paul referred to these "basic principles" or "elemental spirits" (NRSV), he likely had one of two meanings in mind. He might have been referring to the Greek notion of the elements of earth, wind, water, and fire, from which the Greeks believed the material world was built. These elements were often viewed as in opposition to one another. This understanding would be preferred if the Colossians were primarily Greek or Roman in their mindset. What is more likely is that Paul was referring to the Jewish understanding of "basic principles" or "elemental spirits" (NRSV). Jews often viewed supernatural powers in a demonic sense. Thus Paul would be attributing these false teachings to the influence of demonic supernatural powers.

Paul's intention was simply to compare the emptiness of the false teaching with the fullness of Christ. The things promised by the false teachers could not compare to what Christ had already done. Christ, unlike the false teachers, is not empty but is filled with the "whole fullness of deity" (2:9). Not only is Christ not empty, but we ourselves, if we have embraced Christ, are filled with Christ. (2:10).

This comparison between an empty teaching and a Savior who is filled with deity—and also the believers who are filled with this Savior—was Paul's way of encouraging the Colossians that Christ alone is sufficient. Christ alone has truth that is divine in origin. Those who believe have access to this truth because Christ fills them. There is no need for anything external.

We might imagine at this point the false teachers protesting, *But what of the requirements of the law?* Paul directly addressed two of these requirements, the requirement of circumcision and the requirement that law breakers are accountable for their crimes. Paul first said that we Christians have been spiritually circumcised in Christ. At the point that we embrace Christ, we put off "the sinful nature" (2:11). Christ thus removes our spiritual impurities. This removal is symbolized in our baptism as we proclaim that we have died to sin with Christ and been raised as new creatures with him. Paul went on to say that, through Christ's death, Christ made himself accountable for the laws we have broken.

Paul then used the imagery of our sins being written down and nailed to the cross of Christ (2:13–15). He was referring to the Roman custom of writing the offense committed by the accused on a board and nailing it above their heads on their crosses. Our offense became Christ's offense, and his punishment freed us from our accountability under the law.

Paul had made clear his main ideas. Now he was ready to address the specific manifestations of the problem in Colosse.

Rituals and Practices Are No Substitute for the Presence of Christ (2:16–18a)

Paul made it clear that one of the primary problems in Colosse was an emphasis on strict religious practices that included the observance of Jewish food laws and of Jewish festival days. The reference in this section to "a religious festival, a New Moon celebration or a Sabbath day" (2:16) refers to Jewish laws governing the strict observance of such occasions (see 1 Chronicles 23:31; 2 Chronicles 2:4; 31:3; Nehemiah 10:33).

Paul also referred to the practice of asceticism. Asceticism was the practice of denying the body of material things such as food, clothing, sleep, or other basic human needs. The primary outcome desired by ascetics was that in denying the body they would gain control over it. Paul viewed asceticism as an unnecessary practice. He commented that the type of asceticism that observes strict dietary and cleanliness laws may appear to have wisdom but in the end it does nothing in regard to "restraining sensual indulgence" (Col. 2:21–23).

Paul emphasized also that these things were only a "shadow" (2:17). The actual substance is Christ. In calling ascetic rituals *shadows*, Paul once again declared that these rituals were empty and had no meaning except as they pointed to Christ. A shadow is only the one-dimensional outline of the person who casts it. Its only value lies in its ability to lead the eye back to the person it represents. Paul indicated that now that we have seen Christ and now that he is a part of us, we have little need for the shadow.

You may believe that Paul is not speaking to you because you are not seeking to live by Jewish laws. You worship on Sunday, and you have never celebrated Passover. Yet Paul is referring to anything that takes the place of Christ. Some of us have spent years doing our daily Bible reading. We wake up every morning, read our passage for the day, say our usual prayer, and then go on about our day. We would not miss this time for anything. But deep inside we know that our time has become hollow and empty. We feel that we are simply going through the motions, and we wonder whether it is even possible for us to truly connect with Christ. What was once a truly rewarding way to experience the presence of Christ has become a dry ritual. Many similar things can take the place of Christ in our lives. Can such things as church attendance, a certain worship style, and participation in church programs become the objects of our devotion rather than point us to Christ?

Supernatural Powers Are No Substitute for the Presence of Christ (2:18b–23)

Believing in the supernatural has become trendy for many in our generation. Paul dealt with this trend in the form of the false teacher who practiced the "worship of angels" (Col. 2:18). Such a man went on in great detail about divine visions. His mind was puffed up with empty notions. Paul's counter to this teaching was that this false teacher placed his faith in spiritual beings that were in fact beneath Christ. Followers of this teaching had in effect cut off the head, and the body had become useless. Paul encouraged them to remember again that Christ has power over all lesser beings, that he is the ruler and authority, and that there is no need to look to angels, elemental spirits, or mystical experiences apart from Christ himself. If we have direct access to Christ, we have no need for these other things.

We need to think hard about this last point the next time we are tempted to speak about our guardian angel or to desire or promote a fantastic spiritual experience. Paul warns us that without Christ such experiences are hollow and empty. True spirituality does not depend on the latest guru or the most up-to-date devotional experience. True spirituality involves staying connected day-by-day, hour-by-hour to Christ. The latest gimmick will pass. Christ remains.

Implications and Actions

The problem Paul addressed in Colossians was that the church was about to trade the truth of Christ for a lie of human origin. But Paul's bottom line was that Christ alone in us is sufficient for us. We do not need the latest gimmick or the most ancient law in order to be truly spiritual. For Paul, true spirituality rests in our connection to Christ.

When we embrace Christ, Christ fills us with his presence, forgives us of our transgressions, and begins an eternal relationship with us. Our daily encounters with Christ, not our religious checklists or our human insights, determine our spiritual health.

GNOSTICISM

The debate over what group was responsible for the false teaching in Colosse has at times focused on the existence of Gnosticism within the Colossian church. Gnosticism included belief in a secret knowledge that was imparted only to a select group. One tenet of Gnostic belief was that the material world was evil and the spiritual world was good. This belief caused Gnostics to fall into two groups, one group that allowed for indulgence and another group that required asceticism. While some of the elements of Gnosticism seem to have existed in Colosse, recent scholarship indicates that Gnosticism is a later development.

Thus, what is evident in the Colossian church would be pre-Gnostic or would simply have some similarity with later Gnostic thought. It is important to note that Gnosticism blends so many different belief systems that it becomes easy to equate many heresies with it.

SHOULD CHRISTIANS ENGAGE IN SUPERSTITIOUS PRACTICES?

Sally was not sure what to do. She had been meeting with a group of friends regularly at the local coffee shop for months. This particular day was different. The group had decided to invite a tarot card reader to join them and have their cards read. Sally had protested at first, but her friends insisted that it was only for fun. After all, Sally was a spiritual person; maybe she would really connect with God in her reading. Sally had to admit she was fascinated by this suggestion, and so she had shown up for the reading. While sitting there waiting her turn, she was not sure she had made the right decision. If you were in Sally's shoes, what would you do?

QUESTIONS ————————————————

1. What are the things that you do daily to connect with Christ?

2. When you do the things that connect you to Christ, do you have the sense that you are just going through the motions? What does this say about your relationship with Christ?

3. Can you identify three trends that are common in the church today? Do these trends honor Christ, or do they point the believer toward something other than Christ?

4. Can you identify three superstitions, supernatural beliefs, or mystical practices that are seen as acceptable in the world today? Do you believe that these practices point people to or away from Christ?

5. Is American culture's emphasis on the spiritual and the supernatural beneficial or detrimental to Christianity?

Our Next New Study

(Available for use beginning December 2008)

THE GOSPEL OF MATTHEW:
Hope in the Resurrected Christ

Lesson 11	Giving His Life	Matthew 26:26–30; 27:11–14, 35–50
Lesson 12	Under the Command of the Resurrected Christ	Matthew 28:1–10,16–20
Bonus Lesson	Jesus and Hurting People	Matthew 25:31–46

Additional Resources for Studying the Gospel of Matthew: Hope in the Resurrected Christ:[1]

Craig L. Blomberg. *Matthew*. The New American Commentary. Nashville: Broadman Press, 1992.

Dietrich Bonhoeffer. *The Cost of Discipleship*. New York: Simon & Schuster, Touchstone Book, 1995 (originally published in German in 1937).

M. Eugene Boring. "Matthew." *The New Interpreter's Bible*. Volume VIII. Nashville: Abingdon Press, 1995.

David Garland. *Reading Matthew*. Macon, Georgia: Smyth and Helwys Publishing, Inc., 1999.

Douglas R. A. Hare. *Matthew*. Interpretation: A Bible Commentary for Teaching and Preaching. Louisville: John Knox Press, 1993.

A.T. Robertson. "The Gospel of Matthew." Word Pictures in the New Testament. Volume 1. Nashville, Tennessee: Broadman Press, 1930.

Frank Stagg. "Matthew." *The Broadman Bible Commentary*. Nashville: Broadman Press, 1969.

Additional Future Adult Studies

Ezra, Haggai, Zechariah, Nehemiah, Malachi: Restoring the Future	For use beginning March 2009
Participating in God's Mission	For use beginning June 2009
Galatians and Thessalonians: Building on a Solid Foundation	For use beginning September 2009

NOTES

1. Listing a book does not imply full agreement by the writers or BAPTISTWAY PRESS® with all of its comments.

How to Order More Bible Study Materials

It's easy! Just fill in the following information. For additional Bible study materials, see www.baptistwaypress.org or get a complete order form of available materials by calling 1-866-249-1799 or e-mailing baptistway@bgct.org.

Title of item	Price	Quantity	Cost
This Issue:			
Ephesians, Philippians, Colossians—Study Guide (BWP001060)	$3.25	_____	_____
Ephesians, Philippians, Colossians—Large Print Study Guide (BWP001061)	$3.55	_____	_____
Ephesians, Philippians, Colossians—Teaching Guide (BWP001062)	$3.75	_____	_____
Additional Issues Available:			
Growing Together in Christ—Study Guide (BWP001036)	$3.25	_____	_____
Growing Together in Christ—Large Print Study Guide (BWP001037)	$3.55	_____	_____
Growing Together in Christ—Teaching Guide (BWP001038)	$3.75	_____	_____
Genesis 12—50: Family Matters—Study Guide (BWP000034)	$1.95	_____	_____
Genesis 12—50: Family Matters—Large Print Study Guide (BWP000032)	$1.95	_____	_____
Genesis 12—50: Family Matters—Teaching Guide (BWP000035)	$2.45	_____	_____
Leviticus, Numbers, Deuteronomy—Study Guide (BWP000053)	$2.35	_____	_____
Leviticus, Numbers, Deuteronomy—Large Print Study Guide (BWP000052)	$2.35	_____	_____
Leviticus, Numbers, Deuteronomy—Teaching Guide (BWP000054)	$2.95	_____	_____
Joshua, Judges—Study Guide (BWP000047)	$2.35	_____	_____
Joshua, Judges—Large Print Study Guide (BWP000046)	$2.35	_____	_____
Joshua, Judges—Teaching Guide (BWP000048)	$2.95	_____	_____
1 and 2 Samuel—Study Guide (BWP000002)	$2.35	_____	_____
1 and 2 Samuel—Large Print Study Guide (BWP000001)	$2.35	_____	_____
1 and 2 Samuel—Teaching Guide (BWP000003)	$2.95	_____	_____
1 and 2 Kings: Leaders and Followers—Study Guide (BWP001025)	$2.95	_____	_____
1 and 2 Kings: Leaders and Followers Large Print Study Guide (BWP001026)	$3.15	_____	_____
1 and 2 Kings: Leaders and Followers Teaching Guide (BWP001027)	$3.45	_____	_____
Job, Ecclesiastes, Habakkuk, Lamentations: Dealing with Hard Times—Study Guide (BWP001016)	$2.75	_____	_____
Job, Ecclesiastes, Habakkuk, Lamentations: Dealing with Hard Times—Large Print Study Guide (BWP001017)	$2.85	_____	_____
Job, Ecclesiastes, Habakkuk, Lamentations: Dealing with Hard Times—Teaching Guide (BWP001018)	$3.25	_____	_____
Psalms and Proverbs: Songs and Sayings of Faith—Study Guide (BWP001000)	$2.75	_____	_____
Psalms and Proverbs: Songs and Sayings of Faith—Large Print Study Guide (BWP001001)	$2.85	_____	_____
Psalms and Proverbs: Songs and Sayings of Faith—Teaching Guide (BWP001002)	$3.25	_____	_____
Mark: Jesus' Works and Words—Study Guide (BWP001022)	$2.95	_____	_____
Mark: Jesus' Works and Words—Large Print Study Guide (BWP001023)	$3.15	_____	_____
Mark:Jesus' Works and Words—Teaching Guide (BWP001024)	$3.45	_____	_____
Jesus in the Gospel of Mark—Study Guide (BWP000066)	$1.95	_____	_____
Jesus in the Gospel of Mark—Large Print Study Guide (BWP000065)	$1.95	_____	_____
Jesus in the Gospel of Mark—Teaching Guide (BWP000067)	$2.45	_____	_____
Luke: Journeying to the Cross—Study Guide (BWP000057)	$2.35	_____	_____
Luke: Journeying to the Cross—Large Print Study Guide (BWP000056)	$2.35	_____	_____
Luke: Journeying to the Cross—Teaching Guide (BWP000058)	$2.95	_____	_____
The Gospel of John: The Word Became Flesh—Study Guide (BWP001008)	$2.75	_____	_____
The Gospel of John: The Word Became Flesh—Large Print Study Guide (BWP001009)	$2.85	_____	_____
The Gospel of John: The Word Became Flesh—Teaching Guide (BWP001010)	$3.25	_____	_____
Acts: Toward Being a Missional Church—Study Guide (BWP001013)	$2.75	_____	_____
Acts: Toward Being a Missional Church—Large Print Study Guide (BWP001014)	$2.85	_____	_____
Acts: Toward Being a Missional Church—Teaching Guide (BWP001015)	$3.25	_____	_____

Romans: What God Is Up To—Study Guide (BWP001019)	$2.95	_____	_____
Romans: What God Is Up To—Large Print Study Guide (BWP001020)	$3.15	_____	_____
Romans: What God Is Up To—Teaching Guide (BWP001021)	$3.45	_____	_____
1, 2 Timothy, Titus, Philemon—Study Guide (BWP000092)	$2.75	_____	_____
1, 2 Timothy, Titus, Philemon—Large Print Study Guide (BWP000091)	$2.85	_____	_____
1, 2 Timothy, Titus, Philemon—Teaching Guide (BWP000093)	$3.25	_____	_____
Hebrews and James—Study Guide (BWP000037)	$1.95	_____	_____
Hebrews and James—Teaching Guide (BWP000038)	$2.45	_____	_____
Revelation—Study Guide (BWP000084)	$2.35	_____	_____
Revelation—Large Print Study Guide (BWP000083)	$2.35	_____	_____
Revelation—Teaching Guide (BWP000085)	$2.95	_____	_____

Coming for use beginning December 2008

Matthew: Hope in the Resurrected Christ—Study Guide (BWP001060)	$3.25	_____	_____
Matthew: Hope in the Resurrected Christ—Large Print Study Guide (BWP001061)	$3.55	_____	_____
Matthew: Hope in the Resurrected Christ—Teaching Guide (BWP001062)	$3.75	_____	_____

Cost of items (Order value) _____

Shipping charges (see chart*) _____

TOTAL _____

Standard (UPS/Mail) Shipping Charges*	
Order Value	Shipping charge
$.01—$9.99	$6.00
$10.00—$19.99	$7.00
$20.00—$39.99	$8.00
$40.00—$79.99	$9.00
$80.00—$99.99	$12.00
$100.00—$129.99	$14.00
$130.00—$149.99	$18.00
$150.00—$199.99	$21.00
$200.00—$249.99	$26.00
$250.00 and up	10% of order value

*Plus, applicable taxes for individuals and other taxable entities (not churches) within Texas will be added. Please call 1-866-249-1799 if the exact amount is needed prior to ordering.

Please allow three weeks for standard delivery. For express shipping service: Call 1-866-249-1799 for information on additional charges.

YOUR NAME   PHONE

YOUR CHURCH   DATE ORDERED

MAILING ADDRESS

CITY   STATE   ZIP CODE

MAIL this form with your check for the total amount to
BAPTISTWAY PRESS, Baptist General Convention of Texas,
333 North Washington, Dallas, TX 75246-1798
(Make checks to "Baptist Executive Board.")

OR, **FAX** your order anytime to: 214-828-5376, and we will bill you.

OR, **CALL** your order toll-free: 1-866-249-1799
(M-Th 8:30 a.m.-6:00 p.m.; Fri 8:30 a.m.-5:00 p.m. central time),
and we will bill you.

OR, **E-MAIL** your order to our internet e-mail address:
baptistway@bgct.org, and we will bill you.

OR, **ORDER ONLINE** at www.baptistwaypress.org.

We look forward to receiving your order! Thank you!

Moving - Me
Amy - Connie's daughter
Kathy - (Jim's wife)
Shirley - Reeves - Ron